Digital Tools for Knowledge Construction in the Secondary Grades

Digital Tools for Knowledge Construction in the Secondary Grades

Michael Blocher

ROWMAN & LITTLEFIELD
Lanham • Boulder • New York • London

Published by Rowman & Littlefield
A wholly owned subsidiary of The Rowman & Littlefield Publishing Group, Inc.
4501 Forbes Boulevard, Suite 200, Lanham, Maryland 20706
www.rowman.com

Unit A, Whitacre Mews, 26-34 Stannary Street, London SE11 4AB

Copyright © 2016 by Rowman & Littlefield

All rights reserved. No part of this book may be reproduced in any form or by any electronic or mechanical means, including information storage and retrieval systems, without written permission from the publisher, except by a reviewer who may quote passages in a review.

British Library Cataloguing in Publication Information Available

Library of Congress Cataloging-in-Publication Data

Names: Blocher, Michael, author.
Title: Digital tools for knowledge construction in the secondary grades / Michael Blocher.
Description: Lanham, Maryland : Rowman & Littlefield, 2016. | Includes bibliographical references.
Identifiers: LCCN 2016023171| ISBN 9781475828467 (cloth : alk. paper) | ISBN 9781475828474 (pbk. : alk. paper) | ISBN 9781475828481 (electronic)
Subjects: LCSH: Education, Secondary—Computer-assisted instruction. | Educational technology. | Student-centered learning.
Classification: LCC LB1044.87 .B6 2016 | DDC 371.33/44678—dc23 LC record available at https://lccn.loc.gov/201602317

∞ ™ The paper used in this publication meets the minimum requirements of American National Standard for Information Sciences Permanence of Paper for Printed Library Materials, ANSI/NISO Z39.48-1992.

Printed in the United States of America

Contents

Preface	vii
Introduction	ix
Part 1: Foundations	**1**
Chapter 1: Perspective	3
Chapter 2: Instructional Strategies	15
Chapter 3: Standards and Assessment	27
Part 2: Digital Tools for Learning	**41**
Chapter 4: Technology Operations	43
Chapter 5: Global Digital Citizenship	55
Chapter 6: Communication and Collaboration	67
Chapter 7: Research, Data Collection, and Analysis	77
Chapter 8: Creating and Publishing	91
Chapter 9: Thinking Critically: Solving Problems and Making Decisions	103
Chapter 10: Digital Games for Learning	115
Index	127
About the Author	131

Preface

Often when people think about integrating technology into the classroom, they think about how technology might be *used* within the classroom. One way is when the teacher uses technology for classroom management, such as entering student information, grades or attendance into school networked computer. Another way is when the teacher uses technology to project a presentation of content, as some use SMART Boards. Another way is to have students work at the computer to complete a self-paced instructional program or have students use iPads, tablets, or smartphones to practice skills such as math facts.

The purpose of this text is to provide teachers with some ideas of how to integrate technology into their classroom instruction in ways that support student-centered learning. Technology integration from this perspective is not having the teacher use presentation tools to present information to students. Rather, technology integration from the student-centered learning perspective engages students in learning activities in which they are using digital tools to construct meaningful products. It is through that process that helps them build new, more complex knowledge on their existing knowledge.

An easy way to think about this is to visualize which way the information is flowing. If a teacher is using the SMART Board to present information, it may well help students pay attention However, the information is still moving from the teacher to the students. This puts the teacher at the center of and controlling the learning activity. To be sure, there are times that it is appropriate for a teacher to use technology in this manner, but if the student is using the SMART Board, then the student is more at the center of and controlling the learning activity.

Think about it one step further. When students are using digital tools to create meaningful artifacts that focus on academic content, they must organize their background knowledge and assimilate or accommodate the new information as they construct the digital artifact, whether that be a presentation, movie, or other published product. Student-created digital artifacts can provide products that can be assessed for student achievement when the criteria are properly aligned to academic standards. The focus of this text is to do just that: engage students using digital tools in this manner, thus putting them more in control of and in the center of the learning process.

Introduction

This text is divided into two parts. Part 1 provides a foundation for technology integration into classroom instruction, including a perspective and rationale of student-centered learning, instructional strategies for technology integration, and academic standards and assessment as it relates to technology integration within student-centered learning approaches. Part 2 is structured so that each chapter focuses on a specific topic that provides teachers with information and methods of integrating technology.

Part 2 begins with basic technology operations and global digital citizenship. These topics provide a foundation for the remaining chapters that discuss how students can appropriately use digital tools for learning through communication and collaboration, research, data collection and analysis, publishing, critical thinking, problem solving, and gaming. Each chapter in Part 2 provides a contextually based secondary classroom scenario that illustrates the chapter's topic. The scenarios provide an example of the learners using digital tools that help them achieve secondary-grade–level national standards' objectives/outcomes.

Technology's rapid changes makes writing a text of this nature challenging because the current tools will be replaced with new versions or totally new applications. To help alleviate this the text often refers to software and hardware simply as *digital tools*. However, there are also many examples of specific digital tools, which are identified to provide context.

Therefore, as you read through the text, it's important to remember to think about each tool's concept or function, rather than the specific tool described. If a scenario suggests that students use MS Word, don't think that it has to be that actual product. Think about it as a word processor, or better yet a publishing tool, rather than MS Word. Another example is if a scenario identifies a specific cognitive mapping software (i.e., Inspiration), think about any digital tool that can help them visualize their ideas and organize their thoughts.

Thinking in terms of the concept being discussed rather than a specifically identified digital tool or software title will also help you keep up with technology changes. In other words, you should focus on the purpose of the examples in this text and how they demonstrate technology integration in ways that support student-centered learning rather than the tool itself.

Part 1

Foundations

Part 1 provides an introduction, rationale, and perspective of student-centered technology integration instructional strategies and assessment as it relates to secondary learners.

Chapter 1

Perspective

Today's teachers are expected to understand how to use technology to enhance the learning environment within their classroom. However, technology integration can be defined in many ways and methods: to support and enhance classroom management, instructional delivery, and student engagement.

This chapter will introduce you to technology integration from two opposing perspectives of learning: Objectivism and Constructivism. By comparing and contrasting these two perspectives, an illustration of how a teachers' perspective of learning might impact his or her instructional decisions when integrating technology is provided. As you read through the chapter try to reflect on what you think about learning, how you best learn, and how you think your students can best learn. Think about how the methods you employ might impact what technology tools you might use and how they will be used within your classroom.

PERSPECTIVE OF LEARNING

Educational researchers and writers often disagree on learning theories that describe how students learn best. Because we all have had different learning experiences and learn in different ways, one teacher's perspective of learning often can differ greatly from one to another. A teacher's perspective of learning is based on his or her understandings of learning theories as supported by his or her personal learning experiences. As such, teachers generally approach their classroom tasks and decisions from their perspective of learning and classroom experiences.

Even though many might agree that integrating technology into the classroom can enhance the learning environment, teachers may have different ideas about how to do so. Most would probably agree that teachers need to have a rationale for why and how they are integrating technology: being thoughtful to plan how to best engage their students with the technology tools, rather than simply using technology for technology's sake.

Because one's perspective of learning will impact *how and why* you integrate technology, it's important to understand your perspective. To gain a better understanding of how a teacher's perspective of learning might impact how he or she approaches the classroom, here's an example of opposing perspectives of learning as described by early leaders in the field of educational technology.

Vrasidas (2000) compared two contrasting points of view that we can use to help understand different ways to integrate technology. Figure 1.1 illustrates two opposing perspectives of learning in an objectivism-versus-constructivism continuum.

Figure 1.2 includes elements that might help you think about how these opposing perspectives might impact ones approach to learning. For example, objectivists are more likely to approach learning where the teacher has more responsibility for learning, controls the classroom, and is thus defined as more "teacher centered." On the contrary, constructivists are more likely to approach learning where the student has more responsibility for learning, controls his or her learning, and is defined as more "student centered."

Although there are opposite ends displayed on the continuum, most teachers would describe themselves somewhere between objectivism and constructivism, rather than being at one end or the other. For example, there may be times when a teacher might use an instructional strategy that could be perceived as coming from an objectivist's perspective even though she might consider herself a constructivist. A teacher's approach to learning may not be as black and white as one might think. To help frame technology integration let's compare and contrast these two opposing perspectives from each end.

For the sake of gaining a better understanding of integrating technology, think of them in stark contrast. Although this is overly simplified, it may help you think about your perspective of learning by comparing and contrasting two different points of view. Giving these two perspectives in this simplistic manner will help provide discussion points to help you think about technology integration.

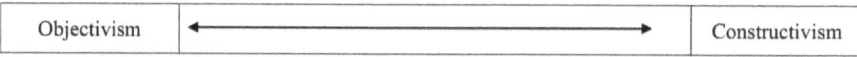

Figure 1.1 Perspective Continuum

Objectivism	←―――――――→	Constructivism
Teacher Centered	←―――――――→	Student Centered
Teacher Control	←―――――――→	Student Control
Teacher Responsibility	←―――――――→	Student Responsibility

Figure 1.2 Teacher-Centered versus Student-Centered

Objectivism

From this perspective, one might believe that knowledge is being cognizant of facts, skills, and concepts as they relate to what is true, making knowledge bound and confined to specifics. Perhaps the main belief here is that knowledge is thought to be a deliverable, which can be transmitted from teacher to student. For example, students gain knowledge of grammar when a teacher provides his or her students with a list of rules for grammar, or students learn fractions after being told and practicing the steps for adding fractions. Often referred to as an *objectivist perspective*, this suggests that knowledge is something that is transferable between the knowledge giver and knowledge recipient.

Constructivism

In contrast, constructivists believe that knowledge is constructed by the student, not received from the teacher, instructor, or computer program. Learning is a much more complex process than simply receiving a set of facts, concepts, or definitions that are simply to be put into memory. Learning is the construction of knowledge, understandings, and skills that students build while engaged in learning experiences where they are thinking about or exploring ideas as they relate to their current understandings.

This viewpoint of learning and knowledge construction is often referred to as a *constructivist perspective* and suggests that human learning is the process of constructing or building new knowledge on the foundation of previous knowledge. From this perspective, the student is responsible for constructing the knowledge. The teacher or instructor is responsible for providing an engaging learning environment that includes support and scaffolds when needed.

Constructionism

When we think about constructivism, especially when we think of using technology tools to promote student engagement, educational technologists often also use the term *constructionism*. Papert (1993) suggests that constructionism supports constructivism but suggests that learning is enhanced when learners are engaged in the *process of construction*. As Papert (1991) stated:

> Constructionism—the N word as opposed to the V word—shares constructivism's connotation of learning as "building knowledge structures" irrespective of the circumstances of the learning. It then adds the idea that this happens especially felicitously in a context where the learner is consciously engaged in constructing a public entity, whether it's a sand castle on the beach or a theory of the universe. (p. 1)

Distributed Constructionism

Resnick (1996) defined *distributed constructionism* in which learners use computer networking technology to support distributed construction through discussions, sharing, and collaborations. In other words, learners benefit from the use of technology that supports collaborative "design and construction activities" (p. 281) to actively engage in the construction of personally meaningful products.

This requires the cognitive engagement of the student, which is more complex than merely constructing new knowledge by engaging in the constructing things. Specifically, Resnick (1996) suggests that, "[w]hat's important is that they are actively engaged in creating something that is meaningful to themselves or to others around them" (p. 281).

Thus, constructionism involves two interactive constructions: the construction of knowledge through the creation of personally meaningful products requiring learners to be cognitively engaged in meaningful learning. From this perspective, constructionism has profound implications for how technology might be integrated into the learning process.

The importance of meaningful learning is echoed by Jonassen, Peck, and Wilson (1999) who provide specific elements of meaningful learning. They suggest that meaningful learning is fostered when students are:

- Actively interacting and being able to observe their manipulating elements within the learning environment
- Constructing individual mental models based upon their experiences and interpretations with prior knowledge
- Intentionally setting goals, selecting strategies, and making decisions about learning
- Authentically situated in some meaningful, real-world task or setting
- Cooperating, collaborating, and socially negotiating within groups working on common tasks

Integrating specific technology tools into the learning environment can support these elements in various ways. For example, interactive visualization software such as Geometer's Sketchpad® provides opportunities for students to manipulate geometric shapes and then observe changes of angles and lengths based on their manipulations. Cognitive mapping tools, such as Inspiration®, support students' constructing mental models of ideas and concepts or to list background knowledge and learning strategies to help them set goals, select strategies, and make decisions.

Internet resources and communication tools can be used to gather data and communicate with experts in the field on topics of real-world issues. Social media and collaborative electronic tools promote cooperation, collaboration, and social negotiations within groups of students as they coauthor papers and reports.

Think about how the technology tools described can support learning as it might relate to how one's perspective of learning can impact how technology might be integrated within the classroom environment.

INTEGRATING TECHNOLOGY

There are several ways that teachers can integrate technology within their classroom. For example, students can learn *about* technology, they can learn *from* technology, and they can learn *with* technology (Jonassen, Howland, Moore, and Marra, 2003).

First, students can learn *about* technology and it is generally described as *computer literacy*. Here students gain understandings that help them use the computer. For example, they would learn how to use the current operating system to navigate the computer to run various applications to create and save files or possibly use the computer to communicate. Understanding the computer and its workings are knowledge and skills that are often defined as computer literacy.

Because technology changes quickly learning about technology is an ongoing process. Even the most highly computer literate people may need to learn about technology at various times. Over the years there have been many substantial changes with new versions of operating systems and productivity tools. Even technology veterans can be left scratching their heads at times. Good problem-solving skills coupled with trial-and-error methods can be invaluable when learning *about* technology.

Second, students can learn *from* technology in which the technology is used to deliver or present instruction or content. When students learn from technology they learn about specific content when presented from the computer, tablet, or even a smartphone. When a teacher uses a presentation tool to create a slide show as a visual aid to support a direct instructional lesson, that is an example of learning from technology.

A better example might be when the student interacts with a computer program, such as in a computer-based instructional (CBI) module. Here students are given specific instruction through a computer programmed with content or activities to help them gain specific knowledge or be able to perform certain skills. These are often self-paced by the learner's ability to answer content questions.

Finally, students can learn *with* technology in which technology tools are used to support and enhance the learning environment. There are many ways that a teacher can engage his or her students with technology tools. The key, however, is that when students learn *with* technology they are generally using technology tools to support their investigation, visualization, or creations that help engage them in the learning process and demonstrate their acquired knowledge.

This is by far the most complex of the three purposes of classroom technology integration discussed because there are many different types of technology tools now available to the classroom teacher, and they can be used in different ways. As you read the next section try to think about how these two perspectives are fundamentally quite different.

Technology Integration from the Objectivist's Perspective

Technology integration from an objectivist's perspective will most probably include the use of technology tools that maintain the viewpoint that knowledge is transferable, which then would include technology tools and software applications that delivers the content to the students. For example, CBI programs are designed to give students specific instructions from a computer programmed with content or activities to help them gain specific knowledge or acquire certain skills.

In some programs students interact with the computer program in a structured linear manner in a way that directs the student through each screen in a specific order, leaving the student little or no control of their learning. Other programs are less linear and provide some degree of student control. The student might be given menus of choice where they select the information, content, or scenarios.

As students select specific topics and go through the material, there can be additional screens that ask the student to interact in some way to demonstrate that he or she has learned that content. These interactions could be in the form of a multiple-choice question, fill in the blank, or click an object and drag it to the appropriate location. More recent and sophisticated programs can even provide for an "intelligent element" that identifies the level of skill or knowledge based on the student's input and then chooses and delivers the appropriate (more difficult or less difficult) level of instruction or interactive activities.

In this way the program guides the student through the learning process at his or her personal learning pace or level. For example, with more input from the student (i.e., clicking on a choice, correct or incorrect answer to a question), the computer program provides remediation, more instruction, or possibly feedback on his or her progress. Even though these programs might provide for greater student control, the instruction is still delivered to the student, and as such, suggests that integrating technology in this manner is from an objectivist perspective.

However, it can be less explicit than that. For example, one might use the Internet, a vast storehouse of content information, to simply deliver information to the student. In this example, the content to be learned would be delivered to students by simply reading the information provided by the Web pages. Although the student has some control over the flow of information, or even perhaps, the type of media that is used to deliver the information, similar to learning from technology described previously, the general flow of information is from the technology tool to the student.

Another example might include multimedia encyclopedias that provide audio and video delivery of content to the student. Software of this nature might even provide interaction in which students are required to engage with the media, clicking on elements within the program that would bring up information or content in various media formats, based on the student's preference. Even though students may have some control over the type and perhaps even the content delivered, they are still recipients, receiving pages of text, narration, or video that provides the information.

Although this is a limited description of the objectivist's perspective of technology integration, it provides a contrasting point on which to discuss the constructivist perspective. As you read through the next section try to remember how the objectivist perspective views knowledge as facts, skills, and concepts and that learning is acquiring or receiving that knowledge from someone or something outside of him or herself. Learning, even with some student control, is still delivered to the student, rather than being generated by the student.

Technology Integration from the Constructivist's Perspective

Technology integration from a constructivist's perspective would most likely require students to be active participants in their use of the technology tools to explore concepts, gather data, test hypotheses, publish and share findings, and thus, generally construct their understandings.

From a distributed constructionist's approach one might engage students where, as members of a team, work together to solve authentic real-world problems by using various technology tools, such as: visualization, exploration, publishing, communication, and perhaps simulations to engage in knowledge construction that can be defined as meaningful learning. Students might be grouped to investigate and provide solutions for real-world problems, such as global warming.

In this example, although students might use Internet resources, it would be for more than simply retrieving information. Here, they would be asked to judge retrieved information for accuracy or reliability. They would analyze findings for accuracy and apply the newly acquired information to help support their conjectures and ideas. They might communicate with experts in the field to gain informed and perhaps differing perspectives on the topic. They might also employ multimedia authoring tools to generate, publish, and share meaningful products as an alternative assessment of their learning.

By integrating technology into learning environments from this perspective, students have the opportunity to work together to assemble and share their understandings of new concepts and ideas as they build on their previous knowledge and thus are learning *with* technology from a constructivist perspective. To integrate technology in this manner, teachers must be able to select technology tools and plan instructional strategies that use these tools in an intentional manner to help their students achieve the objectives or outcomes designed for a lesson.

There are a variety of technology tools that support various instructional strategies and a variety of learning activities, such as practicing, creating, organizing, researching, communicating, exploring, thinking, planning, and visualizing. Integrating technology in this manner means that the teacher must select and plan the use of a specific tool that will best support the learning task. It also means that the teacher must decide on an instructional strategy in which students use that tool within the learning environment in ways that enhance learning and best supports achievement of the objectives, outcomes, or goals for that lesson.

As you might imagine, this can be a complex task that requires sophisticated knowledge of the software and their implementation in learning environments. Maddux, Johnson, and Willis (2001), defined software used in education as Type I or Type II applications. These definitions help teachers understand how software applications differ and why they might select one over another.

Type I Applications

These applications are generally educational software programs designed to provide information to the student. If there are opportunities for student input, it is generally more directed, highly structured, and less open-ended. The software is looking for specific or limited student input. This can be the case even in a simulation tool in which the software developer predetermines almost everything that happens on the screen. Generally, this type of application is aimed at the introduction to or acquisition of facts by rote memory through drill and practice.

A teacher might integrate this type of application to introduce specific concepts to the student, which might be fairly concrete or limited, or have them practice previously introduced skills. As you think about Type I applications, think about the direction of information. In a Type I application, information generally flows toward or is delivered to the student.

Type II Applications

Type II applications generally are more open-ended and require much more active intellectual involvement, in terms of higher level thinking, on the part of the student. These applications may be productivity tools in which students use a tool to create or construct some product that provides them the opportunity to demonstrate their understanding of skills or concepts. The students have much greater control over the interactions between themselves and the computer, which may require unlimited acceptable student input.

These applications are usually aimed at accomplishing more creative tasks than Type I. For example, a teacher might integrate this type of application to support the student in their investigation of information, analysis of data, drawing conclusions, solving problems, and presenting/publishing findings.

As you think about Type II applications, rather than thinking about the direction of information as you did with Type I applications. Think about students using the technology as an intelligent tool to help them build or enhance their knowledge about any particular content or topic. In this way the technology tool could be seen as a collaborator helping and supporting students in the task of learning.

Mindtools

Jonassen uses the term *Mindtools* to suggest that technology tools can be used for constructive learning, stating, "Mindtools are computer-based tools and learning environments that have been adapted or developed to function as intellectual partners with the learner in order to engage and facilitate critical thinking and higher order learning" (2000, p. 9). Technology integration from this perspective engages students in the creative process where they use technology tools to help them construct knowledge.

Mindtools should be used to engage the learner in critical thinking, where they do more than just produce. Mindtools should be used for organizing, modeling, visualizing, constructing, and conversing. For example, word processors are *not* Mindtools, as he defines them because "they do not significantly restructure and amplify the thinking of the learner or the capabilities afforded by that thinking. Word processing does not restructure the task of writing" (2000, p. 16). Although word processors provide an easy to use tool to help one get their ideas onto paper, they don't enhance the student's thinking about what he or she is writing or his or her ability to write well.

Other applications within productivity suites (i.e., MS Office, Open Office, etc.) such as database and spread sheet programs, according to Jonassen, "can also function as cognitive tools for enhancing, extending, amplifying, and restructuring the way learners think about the content they are studying. These applications provide alternative conceptualizations of the content for the learner. They provide new formalisms for thinking. That makes them Mindtools" (2000, p. 16).

Integrating software like Microworlds (i.e., LOGO®) could be considered a Mindtool, because it can provide students with the opportunity to explore, interact, and build scenarios in which they can manipulate variables and observe outcomes. By interacting in this way students can "visually" construct their own individual mental models of complex real-world concepts, thus providing new ways of thinking about them. Communication and publishing software could also be considered Mindtools because they support students working together to assemble artifacts that supports their understanding of concepts as they construct elements adding detail to their mental models.

SUMMARY

The purpose of this chapter was to help you gain a better understanding of technology integration and perhaps its complexity. Teachers are expected to be technologically savvy and proficient at integrating technology to support their classrooms in three ways: classroom management, instructional delivery and student engagement. As such, you should be proficient in using a variety of technology tools for thoughtful purposes in a variety of ways, which requires you to continue learning how to use the ever-growing list of new technologies.

Objectivism and constructivism were presented in contrasting ways to provide explicit and distinct examples to help you better understand how technology can be integrated from a teacher-directed or a student-centered perspective. Although it is an oversimplified way to think about this, the objectivist–constructivist continuum presented might be helpful in thinking about the different ways you might integrate technology.

Classroom teachers should have a rationale for why and how they are integrating technology to best engage their students with the technology tools. Technology integration decisions, like all instructional decisions, should be done thoughtfully. When you integrate technology to present information, knowledge is being transmitted from you to the learner. You are integrating technology in a more teacher-directed manner, in which the teacher is in control of the information dissemination and there are times when using technology to support direct instruction is desired and appropriate.

There will also be times learners can use technology tools to explore new ideas, analyze data, investigate problems, organize information, or present findings; thus, they are engaged in an active way to acquire, assimilate, and construct new understandings and build or enhance skills. In this manner the *learners* are more in control and taking responsibility for their learning. However, integrating technology Type II applications from a constructivist's perspective requires that teachers relinquish the more traditional role of being the giver of knowledge and help the student take on the responsibility for his or her learning.

This chapter compared and contrasted technology integration in terms of the objectivist–constructivist continuum. By offering an overview of these two competing approaches to learning and asking you to reflect on your own philosophy of learning, it is my hope that you gained a broader understanding of the variety of ways you might integrate technology and that you gained understanding of the importance of knowing how and why you might use technology tools within your classroom.

REFERENCES

Jonassen, D. H. (2000). *Computers as MindTools for schools: Engaging critical thinking* (2nd ed.). Upper Saddle River, NJ: Merrill Prentice Hall.

Jonassen, D. H., Peck, K. C., and Wilson, B. G. (1999). *Learning with technology: A constructivist perspective.* Upper Saddle River, NJ: Merrill Prentice Hall.

Jonassen, D., Howland, J., Moore, J., and Marra, R. (2003). *Learning to solve problems with technology.* Upper Saddle River, NJ: Merrill Prentice Hall.

Maddux, C. C., Johnson, D. L., and Willis, J. W. (2001). *Educational Computing: Learning with Tomorrow's Technologies* (3rd ed.). Needham Heights, MA: Allyn and Bacon.

Papert, S. (1991). Situating constructionism. In Idit Harel, *Constructionism* (p. 1). Norwood, NJ: Ablex.

Papert, S. (1993). *The children's machine: Rethinking school in the age of the computer.* New York: Basic Books.

Resnick, M. (1996, July 25). Distributed constructionism. Proceedings of the International Conference of the Learning Sciences, Northwestern University.

Vrasidas, C. (2000). Constructivism versus objectivism: Implications for interaction, course design, and evaluation in distance education. *International Journal of Educational Telecommunications, 6*(4), 339–362.

Chapter 2

Instructional Strategies

Teachers feel and are held responsible for their students learning, but if they believe that students construct knowledge, they must also then provide the freedom for their students to manage and take responsibility for that learning. As you might imagine, each teacher must come to some level of comfort in the balancing act of designing and managing learning activities that provide enough structure to support the students, while at the same time providing the opportunity for their students to construct knowledge.

This may cause teachers to find themselves at an interesting *point of tension* between being responsible for their students' learning and at the same time being able to give students the freedom and opportunity to take control of their learning. Because teachers design instruction or plan lessons, aren't they in control of the learning? If so, then how can teachers provide a student-centered learning environment? Fortunately, there are instructional strategies that classroom teachers use in conjunction with the use of technology tools to help them in that balancing act.

The purpose of this chapter is to describe several instructional strategies as they relate to technology integration. In doing so, you will gain a better understanding of various instructional strategies that will support your instructional decisions as you begin to think about how to organize and manage your classroom and how you will integrate technology into your teaching practice.

INSTRUCTIONAL STRATEGIES

Take a moment to think about the different types of learning experiences that you've had to this point in your life and think about the instructional strategies or approaches to which you've been exposed. For example, as a university student you may have called your university faculty instructors. To help you be more successful learning one of your more difficult subjects you might have hired a tutor. Or, to better perform some specific task or sport you may have worked with a trainer.

Although we may use different terms for each of these types of educators, they all have one goal in common: to improve a student's understanding, knowledge, or skill. However, each of these terms may have a specific connotation, which is often based on how these educators approach their task. As you think about each of these approaches think about how each might be similar or different to that of the teachers you had while attending school from pre-kindergarten to twelfth grade.

Instructor

The term *instructor* is often used to describe one who instructs or imparts knowledge in a systematic way. Indeed, when we think of "reading the instructions" we often think of reading a list of steps to be performed to learn how to operate something. An instructor can provide instruction to individual students, but more often delivers lectures, assigns class homework, requires textbook readings or other resources to a larger group to help them learn the course concepts and content. Although a classroom teacher may often provide instruction, they are generally not called *instructors*.

Tutor

The term *tutor* is often used to describe one who provides more individual help for students who may have specific needs. For example, a tutor may provide individual or small group help for students who have difficulties learning specific concepts or content. Many college students have helped defray some of their college expenses by tutoring some of their peers struggling to prepare for an upcoming test or lab exercise.

By gaining individual help, the student is better able to ask questions and get answers to help them gain an improved understanding of difficult material. Although we don't often think of classroom teachers as tutors, they often act in that manner. Think about how a teacher can provide individual help that is needed at just the right moment.

Trainer and Coach

The term *training* is often used to describe how one gains skills by instruction, discipline, exercise, or drill. For example, the term *trainer* is often used to describe one who helps prepare athletes to perform at a higher level through drill and practice. Similarly, the term *coach* is often used to describe those who help athletes improve their skills by supporting them with direction, feedback, and encouragement. Indeed, gymnastic coaches often provide physical support by holding an arm or leg of their athletes as they begin learning to use the balance beam.

Teacher

The term *teacher* is generally used to describe educators who work with students in pre-kindergarten to twelfth grade. However, there are many times that a classroom teacher may perform many of the roles just described. Teachers act as instructors who design and deliver instruction. They often act as trainers who provide exercises and drills to help improve their students' skills. They also coach their students with supportive encouragement and appropriate comments. Finally, they act as tutors who often provide individual help. Teachers often use various educational approaches that will help their students learn in a variety of ways.

BALANCING ACT AT THE POINT OF TENSION

Let's look at the example of a child learning to ride a bicycle to illustrate how a teacher might act in all of these roles. When a child is learning to move beyond a tricycle to ride a two-wheeler, training wheels are often used. Training wheels are designed to provide stability for the child as they begin learning to ride a bicycle. However, they are designed to be adjustable to allow for various levels of support.

As the child begins to ride the bicycle training wheels can be set at the same level as the main rear wheel. This supports the child in a way that they will not lean nor fall to one side or the other when standing still or just starting out. As the child begins to feel more comfortable and is able to go faster, the training wheels can be raised a bit at a time. This allows the child to begin to take control of the bike, in terms of turning by leaning left or right, but still being balanced. Eventually, they become comfortable balancing the bike to the point that the training wheels are removed as they are no longer necessary.

Although this is a good way to help support the child when they are learning, it is important for the parent to observe and make sure that they are adjusting the training wheels up at the right time. Each child learns to do this at different ages, some more quickly and some more slowly. If, for example, the parent raises the training wheels too soon, the child may lose confidence in his or her ability to balance the bike.

However, unless the training wheels are raised the child will simply ride the bicycle in the same manner that they rode their tricycle. They will not learn to lean the bike to turn, but rather simply turning the handle bars to turn and thus not gain an understanding of the dynamics and balance of riding a bicycle.

In this example, the parent would probably begin teaching their child to ride first by giving their child some *instructions* on the purpose of the training wheels; how they would help the child be stable, how they might begin to ride using them, and how they would be raised as they learned to ride. Next the parent would act as a *coach* by providing support while the child climbs onto the bike and *encouraging* them to be successful.

As the parent observes the child's progress he or she might ask the child if it was time to raise the training wheels. Because every child learns at their own individual pace each is individually *tutored* by his or her parent as they negotiate the raising of the training wheels to the point when they are no longer necessary and the child has been taught to successfully ride the bike.

Similarly, teachers use various educational approaches described here. For example, they often begin by giving their students instructions or directions. They then provide support, scaffolds, resources, and materials. Because some learners learn more quickly than others, the teacher must observe and be aware of their students' individual needs. Then like the parent with the decision of raising or removing the training wheels, teachers must also make decisions that best suit the student's learning.

Teachers want to provide students with the necessary support for their learning, but at the same time give them the freedom to allow them to take control and responsibility of their learning. Some students will need additional scaffolds (i.e., individual *tutoring*, additional practice or resources, *coaching*, and *encouragement*). It is this decision point that creates the *point of tension* for teachers.

Each teacher must come to some level of comfort in the balancing act of designing and managing learning activities that provide enough structure to support the students, while at the same time provide the opportunity for their students to be in control of their learning as they construct knowledge.

TECHNOLOGY INTEGRATION IN A STUDENT-CENTERED APPROACH

Teachers who adopt a more student-centered approach often integrate technology in which students are actively using digital tools to help them construct knowledge. There are several ways in which technology can be integrated that support a student-centered approach. In this section we'll discuss, how to engage students in safe but real-life settings where they work together to produce products, complete tasks, and solve problems as they build and demonstrate their understandings of learning standards embedded within the context of real-life situations through simulations.

In a student-centered approach, technology tools can be used to help students examine a case, make inquiry into topics, collect and analyze data, visualize solutions to a problem, and construct products that demonstrate their understandings. In other words, technology tools are used to engage and support students in research of some kind, analyze their findings, and apply their knowledge and skills to some outcome rather than simply being presented with information and concepts.

Student-centered approaches can still vary in how much structure the teacher provides and how much responsibility is required of the students. The role of the teacher may still vary greatly in terms of the support, resources, and help or scaffolds that must be provided to students in order for them to be successful in this learning environment. As you read through this section, pay particular attention to how you might feel in terms of the *point of tension* as it relates to the methods and strategies described.

Case-Based, Project-Based, and Inquiry-Based Learning

Case-based learning, project-based learning, and inquiry-based learning are instructional strategies that are more clearly defined and considered student-centered. Rather than simply presenting or delivering information and concepts, in these learning approaches students are engaged in research of some kind, analyzing findings, and applying their knowledge and skills to visualize solutions. In doing so, students use technology tools in a similar fashion to those who solve real-world problems in how they identify task assignments, organize work flow, and communicate with peers.

In these approaches, the teacher must still provide information, guidance, and structure, but he or she plays more of a role of facilitator who encourages and expects students to engage in critical and higher-order thinking. The level of structure and guidance often is dependent on the instructional approaches of the teacher in terms of the point of tension.

In case-based learning, the teacher provides a "case" within a context that provides real-life situations. Students are given the opportunity to develop and practice their ability to think critically and to apply the required knowledge and skills to work the case. If the case results in a group or team project, the teacher may provide guidance in teaming strategies by helping the students develop their roles within their groups to facilitate better communication and task completion.

Project-based learning is similar in that students are engaged in activities that require collaboration; however, the activity is more structured and students generally follow procedures or steps to help them work collaboratively to construct a product. In this approach, however, when students encounter problems, the teacher's role is "more likely to be instructor and coach (rather than tutors) who provide expert guidance, feedback and suggestions for 'better' ways to achieve the final product" (Savery, 2006, p. 16).

Inquiry-based learning is probably the most similar to problem-based learning (PBL) in that students are given a question, gather information, and think critically to investigate solutions. Again, the role of the teacher is less like the role of tutor in a PBL approach. Here the teacher can provide direction and information that will help them answer the question at hand. Even though this approach provides more structure or control, the teacher will still need to make instructional decisions that are likely to cause tension.

Problem Based Learning

PBL is similar to case-based, project-based, and inquiry learning. Here students are given an *ill-structured problem* and work in teams to try to find a solution or set of solutions that are based on their research, understanding of theory, and application of knowledge and skills. However, there are fundamental differences, primarily in how much structure is provided and the role of the teacher. "While cases and projects are excellent student-centered instructional strategies, they tend to diminish the learner's role in setting the goals and outcomes for the problem" (Savery, 2006, p. 16). "Characteristics of PBL, include: a) the role of the tutor as a facilitator of learning, b) the responsibilities of the learners to be self-directed and self-regulated in their learning, and c) the essential elements in the design of ill-structured instructional problems as the driving force for inquiry" (p. 15).

The selection of the ill-structured problem is a key element because it is at the foundation to the PBL approach. The problem presented to the students should be real world in that there are no defined solutions and thus requires greater inquiry and engagement into the topic to develop a solution. If the problem is too structured, the students may be less apt to engage fully. Because the PBL approach focuses on the student being responsible and self-directing his or her learning, the role of the teacher becomes critical as well. In a PBL the teacher guides the learning process and provides a debriefing in the role of *tutor*.

Being an effective tutor when using a PBL approach places the responsibility of learning on the students. In addition to gathering information and answers or helping to solve the problem, students are also given responsibility for group organization, role and task assignments, and to plan all of the elements, including selecting the technology tools for research, analysis, and presentation. As a *tutor* within a PBL, the teacher is less directive and simply provides a mirror for students to help them see their thinking processes and help them reflect on the problem-solving process.

As you might imagine, this approach requires considerable support materials and scaffolds to be available for the students in several skill areas. In particular, it quite probably will include scaffolds in teaming, self-directed or self-regulated learning, and of course problem solving (Savery, 2006). As technology is integrated into the PBL, students quite probably will also need scaffolds in information on what technology tools might be best to use for a specific task and skills on using the tools.

Making the transition of being the knowledge giver to that of tutor who helps facilitate learning in a PBL is challenging (Ertmer and Simons, 2006) and deciding and providing the appropriate scaffolds when implementing this approach is likely to cause the point of tension for the classroom teacher.

Collaborative and Cooperative Learning

A student-centered approach often uses collaborative learning or cooperative learning methods. There are varying descriptions and details of how collaborative and cooperative learning differ. For example, Roschelle and Teasley (1995) state that collaboration suggests that students coordinate to accomplish a task.

Cooperation, on the other hand, requires that tasks are partitioned where each individual is responsible for some aspect that builds to the whole of the project or task. Panitz (1996) suggests that cooperation is when students work together within a structured learning environment that supports the completion of an end product or task. Collaboration, on the other hand, is viewed as a personal lifestyle or philosophy. Slavin (1997) views cooperative learning as it relates to ill-structured domains and collaboration as it more relates to well-structured domains.

However, there are common elements that have been identified that exist between the two. The commonalities are:

- learning takes place in an active mode;
- the teacher is more a facilitator than a "sage on the stage";
- teaching and learning are shared experiences between teacher and students;
- students participate in small-group activities;
- students must take responsibility for learning;
- discussing and articulating one's ideas in a small-group setting enhances the ability to reflect on his or her own assumptions and thought processes;
- students develop social and team skills through the give-and-take of consensus-building;
- students profit from belonging to a small and supportive academic community; and
- students experience diversity which is essential in a multicultural democracy (Matthews, Cooper, Davidson, and Hawkes, 1995, pp. 34–40).

With that in mind, however, let's take a look at some of the important elements that are essential for good design of cooperative learning activities. Roseth, Garfield, and Ben-Zvi (2008) argue that the most important aspect of implementing a cooperative learning activity is in providing the instructions of how and what your students are to do. Specifically, they suggest that the instructor group the students, provide specific criteria to successfully complete the activity, and provide structure that connect individual students to the activity goals.

When grouping students, group size can be a crucial element. Groups could range from two to six, but generally work best if they are smaller not larger. Remember the old adage, "Too many cooks spoil the broth." However, groups should be large enough to complete the activity. Think about the tasks that you need to have completed in the cooperative learning task and how long it might take to be completed. Think about how many students might be the best number to work together on it.

You probably have been grouped in cooperative learning activities where you ended up doing the lion's share of the work, or perhaps you may have felt guilty for not doing your fair share of the work. This probably happens much more often than not. Although some students may have the ability to manage groups by creating their own roles and identifying responsibilities to distribute the workload, many do not. Linking individual students to specific products or tasks can be vital if you want to ensure an equitable workload in completing the cooperative learning activity.

By designing *individual accountability* into your cooperative learning activity, you make each member of the team responsible for some element of the final product. Making each individual accountable for some aspect or element of completing the task provides the structure that helps the students know what needs to be done and who will do what. For example, you might want to design specific roles or jobs that are responsible for specific tasks that will help build into the final completed project.

While making students in a cooperative learning group individually accountable, it is also important to ensure that they cooperate with one another. The point of a cooperative learning activity is for students to work together cooperatively. In other words, they depend on each other in their team. By designing *positive group interdependence* into your cooperative learning activity, you require the team to work together to complete the learning task.

You may want to provide the structure that will help them work together to be successful by making it clear that each person in the team is responsible for learning the material in the learning activity *but* also for helping their teammates learn as well. By designing an activity where each individual student's task is part of the final completed project, students must work together to assemble the completed project from the individual parts. In addition, by providing some element of motivation for the success of the entire team helps students see their responsibility for cooperating and helping their fellow students.

PROVIDING HELP AND SUPPORT: SCAFFOLDS

When students work together, they may often need help in a variety of ways, including organizing their teams, getting ideas on the best way to approach their line of inquiry, analyzing, and sharing their findings, not to mention understanding concepts or using a technology tool. This is generally called providing scaffolds, the term *scaffold* was first coined by Wood, Bruner, and Ross (1974). It has been used to describe assistance or tutoring to help support students gain an understanding that they might not otherwise attain.

Similar to the training wheel example used previously, scaffolds are provided by the teacher or a peer while students are just learning concepts and tasks. Once the student has an understanding of the material, they are no longer needed and then not provided. Scaffolds are often necessary in student-centered activities when students need support in a variety of ways. In particular, when integrating technology, students might need to have what Saye and Brush (2002) suggest, "[h]ard scaffolds are static supports that can be anticipated and planned in advance based on typical student difficulties with a task" (p. 81).

Educational software may have hard scaffolds built into the application, in terms of particular tools that students might use to gain support when having anticipated difficulties or additional needs. For example, a multimedia learning program may include links to tools that help students organize and prioritize information. This type of scaffold might help them structure the information so they can gain a better understanding of the material. However, one could also argue that a hard scaffold might be the use of templates for student-produced products that help structure and guide the student in completing a required task.

In addition to hard scaffolds, Saye and Brush (2002) state that "soft scaffolds are dynamic and situational. Soft scaffolding requires teachers to continuously diagnose the understandings of learners and provide timely support based on student responses" (p. 82). Because this type of scaffolding is context- and situation-specific, it could be more difficult to provide; but if given in a timely fashion, it will support the student at their time of need. However, this type of scaffolding is dependent on teachers who can identify and analyze a student's or a team's needs based on a student's question, response, or perhaps just a keen observation.

This form of scaffolding may require the teacher to act as an instructor, tutor, or coach. In doing so, the teacher may need to provide instruction, advice, facilitate ideas, or point the student or a group of students to resources or hard scaffolds that will help them be more successful in completing the task, solving the problem, working in cooperation, or demonstrating the knowledge they've gained.

SUMMARY

The purpose of this chapter is to describe several instructional strategies as they relate to technology integration. Various instructional strategies were discussed in terms of the balancing act in the point of tension between teacher-directed and student-centered learning as it relates to technology integration. Although each teacher will most likely make instructional decisions based on their personal ideas of learning, it is important to understand that all instructional decisions have implications for the student and the teacher.

By adding more structure and taking more control away, students will not be as responsible for their learning, but then they will probably not need as much support to complete the learning tasks. For example, when integrating technology from a structured instructional approach you might define group roles and tasks and outline the activity, require specific technology tool(s) for students to collect, organize, analyze, and share their findings in a specific manner, or provide templates that students follow to create all of their technology-produced artifacts.

However, because students would not be responsible for planning, structuring, and designing their meaningful products, they will also miss discussing and deciding on their team's organization, technology tools to use to gather, organize, or analyze their data. In addition, students will miss the opportunity to think about their learning and to think about how they might use a technology tool that best supports constructing new ideas and concepts as they construct their meaningful product that will best present their findings.

By providing less structure, students will have to take more responsibility for their learning, in terms of having to identify and organize group roles and tasks and outline the activity, select specific technology tool(s) to collect, organize, and analyze data, and identify, learn, and use technology tools to help them produce artifacts that demonstrates their newly constructed knowledge; indeed, the students would have greater control over the many aspects of learning.

This approach will require you to provide more soft scaffolds, such as individual tutoring, mini-lessons, and individualized resources. In this manner you will need to provide support by acting as a partner in the learning process alongside the student, perhaps as instructor, trainer, coach, and tutor. However, in these roles you, as the teacher, can pose thought-provoking questions to help support their critical thinking about how to create a meaningful product that best presents their findings and what things they would need to tell the audience about their findings to get their story thoroughly presented.

As you can see, there are various ways teachers might approach their teaching and how they might integrate technology and various instructional strategies that students might employ. However, it is important to remember that the teacher's decisions can profoundly impact his or her students' learning experience. When thinking about integrating technology within some of these instructional strategies in your classroom, think about some of the elements that you will have to consider. What is your comfort level in terms of the *point of tension* between being responsible for your students' learning and giving them the opportunity to take control and responsibility for their learning? What types of scaffolds, support, and resources might you need to provide your students, in terms of requisite background knowledge, group work, organizing and managing their learning, and technology skills? Finally, but most importantly, how can you best serve your students' learning needs?

REFERENCES

Ertmer, P. A., and Simons, K. D. (2006). Jumping the PBL implementation hurdle: Supporting the efforts of K–12 teachers. *The Interdisciplinary Journal of Problem-based Learning*, *1*(1), 40–54.

Matthews, R. S., Cooper, J. L., Davidson, N., and Hawkes, P., (1995). Building bridges between cooperative and collaborative learning. *Change, 27*, 34–40.

Panitz, T. (1996). A definition of collaborative versus cooperative learning. *Deliberations*. Available: http://www.londonmet.ac.uk/deliberations/collaborative-learning/panitz-paper.cfm

Roschelle, J., and Teasley, S. (1995). The construction of shared knowledge in collaborative problem solving. In C. E. O'Malley (ed.), *Computer supported collaborative learning.* (pp. 69–197). Berlin: Heidelberg.

Roseth, C. J., Garfield, J. B., and Ben-Zvi, D. (2008). Collaboration in learning and teaching statistics. *Journal of Statistics Education, 16*, no. 1. Available: http://www.amstat.org/publications/jse/v16n1/roseth.html.

Savery, J. R. (2006). Overview of problem-based learning: Definitions and distinctions. *The Interdisciplinary Journal of Problem-based Learning, 1*(1), 9–20.

Saye, J. W., and Brush, T. (2002). Scaffolding critical reasoning about history and social issues in multimedia-supported learning environments. *Educational Technology Research and Development, 50*(3), 77–96.

Slavin, R. E. (1997). *Educational psychology: Theory and practice* (5th ed.). Needham Heights, MA: Allyn & Bacon.

Wood, D., Bruner, J., and Ross, G. (1974). The role of tutoring in problem solving. *Journal of Child Psychology and Psychiatry, 17*, 89–100.

Chapter 3

Standards and Assessment

Before the educational standards-based movement, teachers decided what his or her students would learn, which was generally based on district agreed-on grade and discipline curriculum. Beginning in the late 1980s, academic standards were identified to provide standardized outcomes that students should know and be able to do in the various disciplines at specific grade levels, regardless of district or teacher. Adopting specific discipline and grade-level standards was seen as a way to ensure that students would achieve the identified outcomes of those standards.

This chapter will provide a brief overview of current national standards and focus on how teachers might assess student achievement of academic standards based on the digital artifacts that their students create. As such, it is important to remember that this chapter will not provide details on all aspects of assessment—there are textbooks devoted entirely to the topic of assessment—these should be considered for more depth on the topic.

ACADEMIC STANDARDS

Although one might imagine that standards would be "standardized," indeed, there are quite a few national and international organizations, state governments, and even the federal government that have identified standards and it has become a politically charged topic. While various educational standards might be similar, designing them begs several questions: What knowledge, skills, and understandings should our children have? Who should decide those? How will we know if our students have achieved them? What can be done if they don't?

The biggest change in the standards-based education reform happened in 2002, when No Child Left Behind (NCLB) legislation (Elementary and Secondary Education Act, 2015) was enacted nationally. NCLB combined the notion of having academic standards that defined what our children should know and required state-designed assessments to provide accountability, with penalties for schools that did not meet the prescribed levels of success.

To fulfill NCLB, states defined state educational standards, often derived from the discipline standards, but then also created an assessment that would then be aligned to the states' standards. Therefore, because many states were in the process of developing their own assessment, many then developed their own standards, which would be aligned directly to the assessment test.

The process of designing standards and assessments is quite complex. Once standards have been defined, achievement outcomes need to be listed and then *performance indicators* for those outcomes need to be identified to ensure that students have achieved those standards. Next teachers must become familiar with and understand the standards and performance indicators for which they are responsible. Then an assessment must be developed that accurately and reliably measures how well a student has achieved the performance indicators.

Not all states' departments of education agree on what the standards should be, nor on how their students might be assessed. One of the biggest challenges of creating academic standards has been agreeing on outcomes that are appropriate for the various grade levels for each of the specific disciplines.

Teachers need to know the state's standards for the grade level and discipline for which they teach because students are assessed and need to be ready to take the test a state requires. To help prepare students, teachers should be embedding the performance objectives of the various standards in their lessons. This is generally done by breaking down the standards and then designing lessons and units that will help them learn and achieve the performance indicators within those standards. This can be a bit confusing, but here is a way to think about it simply. Of course a lot of details must be filled in, but it really boils down to these three questions.

1. *What do you want them to learn?* Decide what you want your students to achieve. That is identifying the performance indicators within a specific standard you are planning on teaching.
2. *How will you help them learn that?* Decide how you are going to help your students achieve that. Identify and plan the lesson so that it will help your students achieve that performance indicator (i.e., What instructional methods or strategies will you employ? What materials, technologies or other resources will your students use to help them learn?).
3. *How will you know how much they've learned?* Decide how you are going to know if they've met the performance indicator. Plan your

assessment so that it assesses their achievement of the outcomes accurately and reliably.

National Academic Organizations

Over the years, each discipline has revised and realigned their standards, which were then adopted or revised by states for their own state standards. Here are a few examples.

Beginning with the National Council of Teachers of Mathematics (NCTM) writing their national standards for mathematics in 1989, but they have since been revised and currently the NCTM Principles and Standards guide educators for continued improvement of mathematics education. (NCTM, 2015).

The Standards for the English Language Arts were originally published by National Council of Teachers of English (NCTE) and the International Reading Association (IRA) in 1996 and designed to complement other national, state, and local standards. They were reaffirmed by the NCTE Executive Committee in November 2012 and currently available on their Web site (National Council of Teachers of English, 2015).

The National Council for Social Studies (NCSS) first released Curriculum Standards for Social Studies: Expectations of Excellence in 1994. These were revised and the National Curriculum Standards for Social Studies: A Framework for Teaching, Learning, and Assessment were enhanced in 2013, with the publication that outlines the efforts of fifteen organizations that collaborated to provide guidance to deepen instruction civics, economics, geography and history at the K–12 level. The College, Career, and Civic Life (C3) Framework for Social Studies State Standards (NCSS, 2013), details four dimensions to better support teachers of social studies.

The National Science Education Standards were developed by a wide body of governmental, educational, and public groups and individuals (National Academies Press, 1996, p. 106). In addition, in 2013, the Next Generation (NGSS) was released and included partners such as the National Research Council, National Science Teachers Association, American Association for the Advancement of Science, and Achieve, an independent education reform organization (Achieve, Inc., 2015a).

Common Core State Standards Initiative

To help better standardize and give some common elements that all could agree on, in 2010 the National Governors Association Center for Best Practices (NGA) and the Council of Chief State School Officers (CCSSO), published the Common Core Standards (Common Core State Standards Initiative, 2015). In addition, review and feedback during the development of the

Common Core was provided by the National Education Association (NEA), American Federation of Teachers (AFT), National Council of Teachers of Mathematics (NCTM), and National Council of Teachers of English (NCTE), among other organizations.

The Common Core Standards focus on an integrated model of literacy, suggesting that students should be able to read, write, speak, and listen in English and language arts, which helps them to be literate then in history and social studies, science, and technical subjects. As such the standards are then organized by K–8 and 9–12.

Common Core English Language Arts (ELA)

The Common Core ELA focuses on English, Language Arts, and Literacy in History/Social Studies, Science and Technical subjects. There are four key features for the CCELA:

- Reading: text complexity and the growth of comprehension
- Writing: text types, responding to reading and research
- Speaking and Listening: flexible communication and collaboration
- Language: conventions, effective use, and vocabulary.

Reading is then broken down into three types: foundational skills, literature, and informational text. Foundational skills have four subcategories: Print Concepts, Phonological Awareness, Phonics and Word Recognition, and Fluency. Literature and informational text have four subcategories: Key Ideas and Details, Craft and Structure, Integration of Knowledge and Ideas, and Range of Reading and Level of Text Complexity.

In addition, each has grade-level descriptors. For example, eleventh- and twelfth-grade students should attain *key ideas and details* by being able to "1) Cite strong and thorough textual evidence to support analysis of the text. 2) Determine two or more themes or central ideas of a text and analyze their development over the course of the text, including how they interact and build on one another to produce a complex account; provide an objective summary of the text. 3) Analyze the impact of the author's choices regarding how to develop and relate elements of a story or drama (e.g., where a story is set, how the action is ordered, how the characters are introduced and developed)" (Common Core State Standards Initiative, 2015, p. 38).

Common Core Mathematics

The Common Core Mathematics Standards take a less integrated approach, but were designed to help make the standards and curriculum coherent, as Schmidt, Houang and Cogan (2002) "by stressing conceptual understanding of key ideas, but also by continually returning to organizing principles such as place value or the properties of operations to structure those ideas" (p. 4).

There are two types of Common Core Mathematics Standards: Standards for Mathematical Practice and Standards for Mathematical Content. In the Mathematical Practice Standards students should be able to:

1. Make sense of problems and persevere in solving them.
2. Reason abstractly and quantitatively.
3. Construct viable arguments and critique the reasoning of others.
4. Model with mathematics.
5. Use appropriate tools strategically.
6. Attend to precision.
7. Look for and make use of structure.
8. Look for and express regularity in repeated reasoning.

Each grade level then has its specific content standards that build on prior grade-level learning. For example, "In Grade 8, instructional time should focus on three critical areas: (1) formulating and reasoning about expressions and equations, including modeling an association in bivariate data with a linear equation, and solving linear equations and systems of linear equations; (2) grasping the concept of a function and using functions to describe quantitative relationships; (3) analyzing two- and three-dimensional space and figures using distance, angle, similarity, and congruence, and understanding and applying the Pythagorean Theorem" (Common Core State Standards Initiative, 2015, p. 17).

Issues with Common Core

Each state then had the choice of adopting the Common Core Standards and initially, forty-five states adopted it. At this writing, however, some state departments of education are choosing to "re-brand" or move away from the Common Core completely. Some have concerns regarding the national government taking control of local school curriculum. However, many state departments of education cite a huge concern over the online assessment costs developed by vendors such as the Partnership for Assessment of Readiness for College and Careers (PARCC) consortium (Rix, 2013).

While at this writing the future of the Common Core is unclear, there is an initial attempt to provide a *common* set of K–12 outcomes in English language arts/literacy and mathematics for college and career-ready standards (Bidwell, 2014). Indeed, even NCLB is being reconsidered (Elementary and Secondary Act, 2015).

National Educational Technology Standards (NETS)

There are also technology standards developed by the International Society for Technology in Education (ISTE). As of 2007, they were redefined as the National Educational Technology Standards, labeling them Standards*S for students, Standards*T for teachers, Standards*A for school administrators, Standards*C for technology coaches to help support peers becoming digital educators, and Standards*CSE for computer science educators. The student standards help teachers think about technology outcomes for students, and teacher standards provide outcomes for technology integration (ISTE, 2016).

USING DIGITAL TOOLS FOR ASSESSMENT

Although the standards students meet may vary, depending on state, every classroom teacher will be responsible in helping their students meet some performance indicators. Once identified, instructional and lesson planning can begin. In addition, assessment must be planned to find out what students have achieved or learned. Having students create digital products for assessment can make this a bit more complex. In addition, there are two types of assessments that should be employed, summative assessments and formative assessments.

Summative Assessments

A summative assessment acts as a summation report *of* learning and is designed to assess the student's achievement generally at the end of a lesson, unit, or even a grade level. The summative assessment should accurately measure the student's achievement of the targeted performance indicators. Although a standardized test is an example of a summative assessment, you will also want to design quality summative assessments for your lessons and units that provides information that can be used by you, your students, and others.

However, there are a variety of ways that this can be done. The key is keeping in mind the term *alignment*, meaning that the assessment should *accurately* assess the students to see if they've achieved the performance indicators. Although this might seem pretty straight forward, it is easy to lose track when looking at digital products students create, like a presentation slide show.

Chappuis, Stiggins, Chappuis, and Arter (2012) describe keys to quality assessment, which include:

1. They are designed to serve the *specific needs of intended user(s)*.

2. They are based on clearly articulated and appropriate *achievement targets*.
3. They *accurately measure* student achievement.
4. They yield results that are *effectively communicated* to the intended users.
5. They *involve students* in self-assessment, goal setting, tracking, reflecting on, and sharing their learning (p. 3).

First an assessment should provide specific and detailed information for a variety of people, including you, your students, your students' parents, and your administration. When thinking about designing an assessment it is important to know who will be using the information gained.

Second, the assessment should have *clear targets*, which can also be defined as the performance indicators outlined in the standards discussed in the previous section. When thinking about designing an assessment, being *aligned* to the identified performance indicators for the lesson is key.

Third, the assessment should be well designed, in terms of the criteria accurately matched to the performance indicators. The assessment should be appropriate for the learning task and grade level. The assessment should not be biased and not impacted by another variable.

Fourth, effective communication should provide feedback to intended users on a variety of levels and guide instruction for the teacher and provide feedback for the student for the future. Achievement levels should be tracked and communicated or reported and should accurately indicate achievement.

Fifth, students should be involved in the assessment. In other words, the assessment should provide helpful information to the students. Students should be clearly aware of the assessment criteria or performance indicators. The assessments should allow students to keep track of progress and use the information to reflect on and set their own learning goals.

Formative Assessments

A question that is often asked of new teachers is: *"What would you do if you designed and taught a unit, then gave an end of the unit test and all of your students failed?"* Although it could be that all of the students failed, but why? The problem could have been with the lesson design, the teaching of the lesson, or the assessment. To keep this from happening, teachers often use a *formative assessment* to keep track of the learning progress during the unit, thus reducing the possibility of that happening.

Formative assessments have the specific purpose to improve or enhance learning by clearly communicating the relevant information on the students' progress. Formative assessments can also inform you on how well the lesson was designed or how well it is being taught (i.e., the clarity of a lesson, the efficacy of an instructional strategy, and sufficient practice of complex skills). In other words, a good formative assessment can provide information during the lesson on a student's progress that will help improve the learning environment, which will enhance the student's opportunity to better achieve the objectives or outcomes.

SECONDARY EXAMPLE

Jill, a high school science teacher has identified that her lesson will cover Next Generation Science Standards (HS-ESS3-4) Human Sustainability: Evaluate or refine a technological solution that reduces impacts of human activities on natural systems. The performance indicator for this standard states that students will be able to provide: *Examples of data on the impacts of human activities could include the quantities and types of pollutants released, changes to biomass and species diversity, or areal changes in land surface use* (*such as for urban development, agriculture and livestock, or surface mining*) (Achieve, 2015b).

Jill decides that to best help her students achieve this performance indicator, she will have them work in teams to research human causes of pollution and then create a movie that details their findings and lists steps that humans might take to help alleviate the issue. The movie will serve as the summative assessment product, which will be used to assess their learning. However, this requires well-designed assessment instruments. Let's look at how these five keys impact the way she might design and use two different types of assessment to assess her students' achievement of this performance indicator.

Assessing Learning

Using digital products, such as a movie, to assess student learning can be complex. Assessing the movie could prove complex and students might provide a variety of good examples of human-caused pollution and solutions. Examples for limiting future impacts could range from local efforts (such as reducing, reusing, and recycling resources) to large-scale geo-engineering design solutions (such as altering global temperatures by making large changes to the atmosphere or ocean). Jill decides that a well-designed rubric to assess their work will be an effective assessment instrument, and she considers the five keys to a quality assessment.

To meet the first key her rubric included details that will help everyone understand how it will *serve her and her students' needs*. To meet the second key, she designed her rubric to *clearly articulate the appropriate achievement indicators*. To do this, she copied and pasted the specific standard indicator into the criteria row, so they were directly aligned.

To meet the third key, her rubric needs included appropriate descriptors to *accurately measure* various levels of achievement. She chose to include three of the achievements and for each criteria row, she included appropriate descriptors. To meet the fourth key, her rubric was clear and then shared with her students before engaging in the unit so that the expectations were *effectively communicated*. To meet the fifth key, her rubric needed to *involve students*. In this case, by having her students share their movies they were able to reflect on their team's movie and their learning.

Jill provided her students with the criteria for the content by listing the following:

1. Examples of data on the impacts of human activities causing pollution (i.e., quantities and types of pollutants released, changes to biomass and species diversity, or areal changes in land surface use such as for urban development, agriculture and livestock, or surface mining).
2. Examples for limiting future impacts could range from local efforts (i.e., reducing, reusing, and recycling resources) and
3. Examples of large-scale geo-engineering design solutions (i.e., altering global temperatures by making large changes to the atmosphere or ocean).

In addition, Jill also provided a list of the technical criteria for the movie. Although this was not essential for measuring the outcomes of the NGSS: HS-ESS3-4, Jill wanted her students to know her expectations on the technical elements. Movies must be four to five minutes in length, include narration and background music, include at least fifteen clear and appropriate images and at least one video of experts in the field, include good grammar and spelling for any text, and include a title with authors' names and credits for references and resources.

Collaborative, Team, and Individual Assessments

Jill realized that there was another element that must be considered for this summative assessment. She wanted to be able to assess her students individually while they were working in teams. Cooperative learning has been researched for years with consistent findings. Slavin (1990) suggested that *positive interdependence* between team members (i.e. having group goals) and *individual accountability* provide the structure that supports enhanced student achievement and yet provides methods for individual assessment.

Jill decided to use a *team checklist* to assess the technical criteria to be placed into, which can then be used to provide a score for the technical criteria (see table 3.1). This score becomes a *team score* for the movie, which is given to each team member. Having a team score provides a common goal and supports positive interdependence of working together to do the best they can as a team.

To provide for individual accountability Jill used an individual summative assessment. Each member of the team was given the choice of choosing one of three types of pollution to investigate; air, water, land, or other, which they individually investigated and reported upon within the movie. The movie had three sections, each detailing the impact of that person's pollution type and the steps that humans might take to alleviate that pollution.

The criteria for NGSS: HS-ESS3-4 performance indicators were then used to create an *individual content rubric* to score the content for each individual student's portion of the movie (see table 3.2). By having each student create their own section of the movie requires them to individually research and then demonstrate their achievement, which provided Jill an individual summative assessment for the outcomes of the unit.

Table 3.1

Criteria	10–9	8	7	6–0	Weight	Score
Movie Length (4–5 minutes)					1	
Title with authors' names					1	
Narration					1.5	
Background music					1.5	
Clear and appropriate images (15)					1	
Embedded video of experts in the field					1.5	
References and resources					1	
Grammar and spelling					1.5	

Table 3.2. Individual Content Rubric

Criteria	Approaches 0–69%	Meets 70%–89%	Exceeds 90%–100%	Score
Examples of data on the impacts of human activities causing the identified pollution	There was at least one accurate example that included the quantities and types of pollutants released. Examples although accurate were limited in details on changes and didn't include elements of biomass, species diversity, and/or areal changes in land surface use. Examples although accurate were limited regarding: urban development, agriculture, livestock, and/or surface mining.	There were multiple examples with some details of the quantities and types of pollutants released. Examples included: details on changes to biomass OR species diversity, OR areal changes in land surface use. Examples included: urban development, agriculture OR livestock, OR surface mining.	There were multiple accurate examples that detailed the quantities and types of pollutants released. Examples provided accurate details on changes to biomass and species diversity, and areal changes in land surface use. Examples included accurate details on: urban development, agriculture and livestock, and surface mining.	
Examples for limiting future impacts of the identified pollution from local efforts.	The movie included at least one accurate example of one of the three R's of limited resources. • Reducing, • Reusing, and • Recycling	The movie included at least one accurate example of each of the three R's of limited resources. • Reducing, • Reusing, and • Recycling	The movie included multiple accurate examples of each of the three R's of limited resources. • Reducing, • Reusing, and • Recycling	
Examples of large-scale geoengineering design solutions.	The movie included at least one accurate example of altering global temperatures by making large change to the atmosphere, ocean OR land.	The movie included at least one accurate example of altering global temperatures by making large changes to the atmosphere ocean and land.	The movie included multiple accurate examples of altering global temperatures by making large changes to the atmosphere ocean and land.	

Jill also decided that she would use an additional individual summative assessment. Each student was required to create a final blog posting where they addressed questions directly aligned to the NGSS: HS-ESS3-4 performance indicators. Jill gave students the opportunity to discuss what they learned about human sustainability and what they would like to learn, thus asking them to re-set learning goals on this topic.

Assessing Instruction and Student Progress

As a veteran teacher Jill knew that given the learning task of working in teams to do specific research and then create a movie was a complex task. Regardless of how much structure and scaffolding she provided, she knew that she and her students would benefit from knowing how things were going during the unit.

Although Jill knew she would monitor and observe their progress, she also knew that a formative assessment would provide her and her students with more in-depth specific information, helping them to be successful. Specifically, she wanted to provide the opportunity for them to set goals and reflect on their progress. She had every student create a *reflection blog*, where each day they created a post. Beginning by setting goals, students were then able to self-reflect on how well they were achieving them and made adjustments that enhanced their progress.

Each day's post included a specific sentence stem directly related to the specific criteria that were aligned to the lesson outcomes, such as: "Humans impact the earth by . . . ". These daily reflections provided her with targeted information that helped her understand how well her students were doing and who might need some remediation. She was able to get a quick idea of which of her students were unclear about or completely missing an important concept. Perhaps more importantly, these blog reflections helped her students understand what they have learned and what they yet needed to learn, thus helping them set accurate learning goals.

SUMMARY

Given the high stakes nature of academic standards, NCLB, and assessment integrating technology where students use digital tools for inquiry, investigation, and practice can be quite complex and often requires extensive planning, structure, and scaffolding, depending on the level of the students. It is important for classroom teachers to have a good understanding of academic standards and assessments as they relate to a student-centered learning perspective. When doing so, students use digital tools to create digital artifacts that teachers can use to assess academic achievement of performance indicators as outlined by the various academic standards.

The chapter provided examples that detail how student achievement might be assessed, both in a formative and summative manner when looking at student products created using digital tools. Assessment is a complex topic and the purpose of this chapter was not to cover it completely. The examples provided should be seen as models for assessing meaningful products students create using digital tools. There are textbooks devoted entirely to that topic, which should be referenced for more specific assessment information.

REFERENCES

Achieve, Inc. (2015a). *Next Generation Science Standards: For States, By States. (NGSS)*. Retrieved from http://www.nextgenscience.org/next-generation-science-standards.

Achieve, Inc. (2015b). *Next Generation Science Standards: For States, By States. (NGSS)*. HS-ESS3-6: Human Sustainability. Retrieved from http://www.nextgenscience.org/hsess-hs-human-sustainability.

Bidwell, A. (2014). Common core in free fall. *U.S. News & World Report*. Retrieved from http://www.usnews.com/news/articles/2014/08/20/common-core-support-waning-most-now-oppose-standards-national-surveys-show

Chappuis, J., Stiggins, R., Chappuis, S., and Arter, J. (2012). *Classroom assessment for student learning: Doing it right—using it well*. Upper Saddle River, NJ: Pearson Education, Inc.

Common Core State Standards Initiative. (2015). *Read the standards*. Retrieved from http://www.corestandards.org/read-the-standards.

Elementary and Secondary Education Act. (2015) Retrieved from http://www.ed.gov/esea.

International Society for Technology in Education (ISTE). (2016). *ISTE Standards*. Retrieved from http://www.iste.org/standards/iste-standards/.

National Academies Press. (1996). National Science Education Standards (NSES). Retrieved from http://www.nap.edu/openbook.php?record_id=4962.

National Council for Social Studies (NCSS). (2013). The College, Career, and Civic Life (C3) Framework for Social Studies State Standards: Guidance for Enhancing Rigor of K–12 Civics, Economics, Geography and History. Silver Spring, MD: Author.

National Council of Teachers of English (NCTE) and the International Reading Association (IRA.) (2015). Standards for the English language arts. Retrieved from http://www.ncte.org/standards/ncte-ira.

National Council of Teachers of Mathematics (NCTM). (2015). *Principles and standards*. Retrieved from http://www.nctm.org/Standards-and-Positions/Principles-and-Standards/.

Rix, K. (2013). Common core under attack. *Scholastic, Inc*. Retrieved from: http://www.scholastic.com/browse/article.jsp?id=3758244.

Schmidt, W., Houang, R., and Cogan, L. A. Coherent curriculum: The case of mathematics. *American Educator* (Summer 2002): 4.

Slavin, R. E. (1990). Research on cooperative learning: Consensus and controversy. *Educational leadership, 47*(4), 52–54.

Part 2

Digital Tools for Learning

Each chapter in Part 2 discusses digital tools that can support and assist secondary student learning. In addition, this section provides contextually based secondary classroom examples that illustrate the chapter technology concepts. Each chapter includes a scenario that elucidates integrating the digital tools discussed as they support students achieving specific national standards' objectives and outcomes.

Chapter 4

Technology Operations

Although most are familiar with basic computer functions, technology changes at such a rapid rate, to fully support students, their teachers should have a good understanding of basic computer functions. This chapter will focus on those computer concepts as they can be compared and contrasted to human information processing. It is hoped that comparing the similarities between human information processes and computer processes will provide a metaphor on which to build a better understanding.

HUMANS AND COMPUTERS

Computer hardware and operating systems can be a bit complex or confusing, and some people have difficulties understanding how a computer actually works. Often, however, computer processing concepts are explained in terms of human brain functions, in particular memory. This comparison may provide a scaffold on which to better gain an understanding of technology processes.

Human Information Processing: Multistore Memory Model

Most humans *process information* as defined in the Multistore Model (Atkinson and Shiffrin, 1968). As shown in figure 4.1, first a person hears, sees, or perhaps feels something and experiences some kind of environmental input that goes into the sensory information store. *Attention* is then focused on the sensory input and the brain begins to *process* the information received in short-term memory, also known as *working memory*.

As one thinks about the information, he or she compares and contrasts it to prior knowledge held in long-term memory and *thinks* about how this information relates to what he or she already knows in terms of information and experiences held in long-term memory. If the information is new, it is encoded and sent to long-term memory to be available in the future.

If the new information is complex, however, one might have to retrieve and encode information back and forth several times with past experiences and background knowledge to better understand that sensory input. As one is engaged (paying attention) he or she *processes* the information to the point where it makes sense, builds new, or enhances existing knowledge.

Computer Information Processing

Computers work in a similar fashion, as shown in figure 4.2. When the computer is turned on, *basic input/output system* (BIOS) is activated. The BIOS is imprinted on the computer *motherboard*, which is the main circuit board that connects all of the computer parts. When the BIOS is activated, by turning on the computer, it provides basic information regarding what hardware is connected to the motherboard and most importantly instructs the computer to look for and start the *operating system* (OS), which is Windows, Macintosh, or Linux.

The computer OS Windows, for example, is really just software that is most often stored on the hard drive and is configured in a manner that helps all of the other hardware and peripherals (RAM, hard drives, monitor, mouse, printer, scanners, etc.) function properly. For example, the OS helps the monitor display what users need to see, the mouse to move to select items, and keyboard to enter text to use the computer.

Computer functions can be compared with the sensory information store in human information processing, which is the element that receives input. In

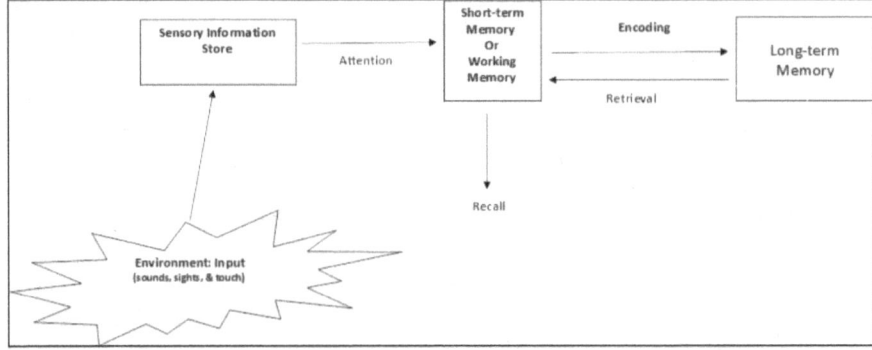

Figure 4.1 The Basic Structure and Processes of the Atkinson and Shiffrin Multi-store Model

the case of the computer, however, the OS is software that sets up communication channels between the various parts and waits for information from the input devices (e.g., mouse or keyboard). Simply put, the OS helps all the computer parts function with one another.

As *input* devices create information (i.e., using a mouse to select an item, using a keyboard to type), the OS receives, organizes, and directs that information to the central processing unit (CPU) to be *processed.* The CPU processing the information could be compared to a person paying attention or thinking about something. This is similar to how a person *processes* things seen, heard, or read and then the brain decides what to do with that information.

In the computer, the OS and the CPU work together to help the computer make sense of all of the information that moves around and through it. This all happens within the computer's random access memory (RAM). RAM is where the computer thinks about all of the information while the computer is *working on something*. RAM is much like the short-term memory in humans because it is a working area in which the computer can temporarily store and work with information. When using a word processor to write a paper, the keystrokes create text on the page that is held in the computer's RAM.

Information held in the computer's RAM is not kept in a permanent fashion and must be saved to the hard drive or some other storage device, much like humans encoding information to long-term memory. This is why if a computer is shut down before the work is saved, it is often lost; RAM is *temporary*. However, if saved to the hard drive or other permanent storage, information can be retrieved to be viewed or edited at a later date.

When information or processes are complex, the computer may function much like a human, encoding and retrieving complex information back and forth between long- and short-term memory. For example, while typing a paper, current word processors can recognize that the user typed a word incorrectly and then retrieves the correct spelling to automatically apply it to the word. The incorrect spelling is only held in RAM, whereas the correct spelling is stored on the hard drive but the word processor and OS work together to move information back and forth to fix the misspelling.

Because people need to be able to see what input they are providing (i.e., typing or mouse movements), the computer also has *output* devices. The most common is the computer screen. However, there are other output devices, such as a printer or speakers. For example, once a paper is written it can be sent to the printer for a hard copy.

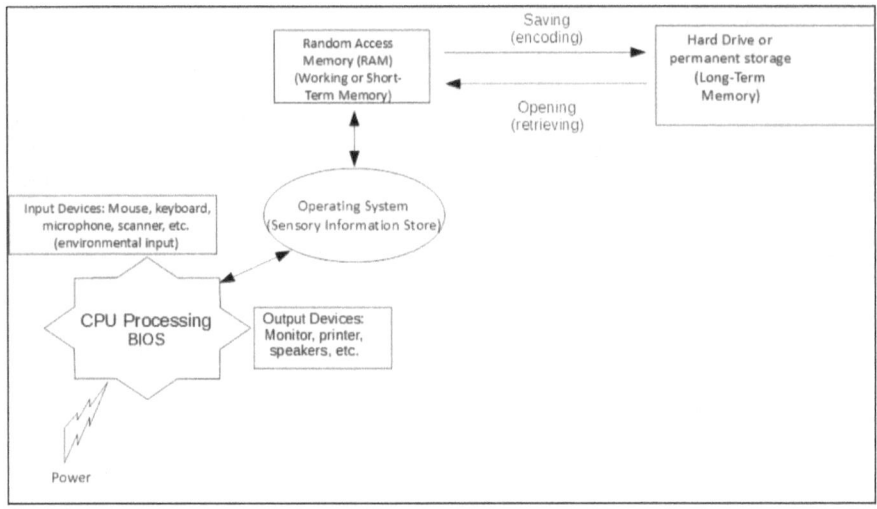

Figure 4.2 Structure and Processes of the Computer

SOFTWARE, FILE STORAGE, AND FILE MANAGEMENT

As mentioned previously, the computer OS is software that organizes and manages the computer. In addition, there are other software applications designed to perform specific tasks and functions. Microsoft Office and Libre-Office include word-processing, presentation, and spreadsheet software and are considered productivity tools. Often times these are installed on a computer when it is purchased or when they are bought and installed by a person later; these are called *computer-based software*.

Some software, such as Google Docs, are not really installed on the computer, but rather can be accessed via the Internet. For example, Chromebook doesn't have any software installed on the computer for the most part. To use it for most any type of word processing, users must be connected to the Internet where they can use the server-based software, Google Docs (Google, 2015). The big difference here is understanding where the software resides, on the computer or on the Internet.

Computer-Based Software

New computers often have quite a bit of software already installed on the hard drive, such as some productivity tools, an Internet browser, an e-mail client, among others. Software designed for specific functions can also be purchased and installed on the hard drive. Some of these can be expensive, but there are also Open Source software applications that can be downloaded and installed, generally for free. These serve the same purpose as expensive software. The key is that if it is installed on the computer, then it can generally be used without being online.

Server-Based Software

There are also software applications that are available, which do not reside on a computer, and many are free. Google Docs is a good example of server-based software and could be described as being on the Google Cloud. Google accounts are free and permit the creation of all kinds of productivity documents similar to, and most importantly, *compatible with*, Microsoft Office (i.e., word processing, presentations, spreadsheets).

Files created in Google Docs are saved online as well. However, files can also be uploaded and downloaded to and from a computer hard drive as well. Google Docs is only one example of the many software applications that are server-based. Indeed, Microsoft's OneDrive (2016b) is comparable to Google Docs. The key here is that without Internet access, you cannot use this type of software.

Open Source Software

Although available for several decades, many folks are not aware of or familiar with open source software. The Open Source Initiative (Open Source Initiative, 2015) supports free computer-based software, which can be downloaded and installed for free. For example, Ubuntu is a free Linux Distribution operating system with the philosophy "that software should be free and accessible to all" (Canonical, Ltd., 2015. para 1).

Developed, delivered, and supported by the Ubuntu Community, this operating system includes additional software such as Foxfire web browser (Mozilla, 2015a) and Thunderbird e-mail client (Mozilla, 2015b). In addition, Ubuntu includes LibreOffice, a productivity tool that parallels Microsoft Office and allows users to open, edit, and then save word documents, spreadsheets, presentations, and others created in Microsoft Office.

LibreOffice (The Document Team, 2015) can also be downloaded and installed onto computers running Apple's Macintosh or Microsoft Windows operating systems. In other words, you do not need to be running the Linux OS to take advantage of other open source software. Other software titles such as Audacity (Sourceforge.net., 2015), which is a free audio recording and editing software, and Gimp (Free Software Foundation, Inc., 2015), an image-editing software that parallels Adobe Photoshop are also available and can be downloaded for free and installed on Linux, Windows, and Macintosh operating systems.

Being knowledgeable about open source software can be a huge advantage for teachers, so that they can provide their students with technology tools, even when their school or district does not have the financial resources to purchase some of the expensive software.

FILE OR DATA STORAGE

When a file is saved, it is saved in the form of a data file in a *storage* area. If the software you are using is computer based, it generally would be saved on the computer's hard drive. When saving a file using server-based software, it would generally be saved on the server where the software resides. Sometimes this can be auto saved, meaning that the server software automatically saves as you work.

Data storage are often compared to a filing cabinet because work or data files are like pieces of paper that can be organized into folders and subfolders. Generally, a computer OS creates some standard folders for specific kinds of files to help one organize their data. There are usually folders called documents, pictures, music, movies, or videos.

Although this is a good way to get started in keeping files organized, it can get more complicated when working in a school computer lab because there are many other options for storage. It is important to understand some of the more complex aspects of data storage and file management in order to be able to find what works in school or other public computer labs.

Local Storage

Local storage is often a term that is used for a computer's hard drive because it is the storage device that is located on the local computer where files can be stored. When writing a paper on a home computer, for example, it will most likely be saved locally on the computer's hard drive. This works well if one is using a specific computer. However, if working in a school computer lab or at a friend's house, files should be saved on *removable* or *network storage*.

Removable Storage

Removable storage is often a good place to save work when working on computers at different locations. There are many types of removable storage currently available to connect to just about any type of computer. Removable or portable USB storage devices come in two basic types and can be an inexpensive option and generally used on just about any computer.

One type is called a portable hard drive. These are usually about the size of a small book, but they can hold a lot of data. This type of portable drive might be good for a classroom teacher who wants to keep a lot of data in one portable location. Others, thumb, flash, or USB drives, are small but can still hold a substantial amount of files or data.

Both portable hard drives and thumb or flash drives are generally good for individual students; they simply plug into the USB port on the computer. This allows a student to carry their files with them from working location to working location. The downside is that a flash drive is so small, it is easily forgotten in the computer lab.

Network Storage or "The Cloud"

Network storage is another option for saving work in a school computer lab. This requires having access to a server where teachers and students can save work over the network. Most schools have a local area network (LAN). The LAN is generally a small network that connects the local computers in the school or computer lab. The LAN is then connected to a wide area network (WAN), which is what provides Internet connectivity.

This type of network configuration provides greater security because it allows local computers to communicate with one another and get information to and from the Internet because it does not let computers outside of the LAN (i.e., in the WAN) connect locally. A network storage area is often *mounted* (or linked) to the local computer so that when you save, you simply locate and select the appropriate *network drive*. Network storage can work well in a school computer lab environment because students can access their own personal storage area from any computer in the computer lab, perhaps school, and even sometimes from their homes.

The Cloud or *Cloud Computing* are terms with which many are familiar. Actually, the cloud is really network storage. The difference is that Microsoft, Apple, and many others have provided network storage on their servers, naming them various names such as iCloud. In addition, they have built-in applications into their OS to help automate the process of backing up music, photos, and other data files. This might be a good option for you, but be aware of where the backups actually are being saved and who might have access to them. Although Google Docs doesn't really call their network storage a cloud, it could be considered one.

File Management

Regardless of the type of storage one uses, it is important to organize files in some logical fashion. Perhaps one of the biggest difficulties people have when using a computer is *not* thinking about managing and organizing their files and just letting it happen haphazardly. It can be extremely frustrating and time-consuming for students if they can't find the file they need.

There are endless ways to organize files, but it is important to find a way that works for you. Some organize their files by file types (i.e., all word documents in one folder, all pictures in another folder, etc.). Others organize their files by date; all files created in a certain period of time are stored in one folder. Still others, organize their files by some relational structure (i.e., all files related to a course go into one folder, whereas files related to another course go into a different folder). It may take a little bit of time to organize your files, but it is time well spent.

USERS WITH SPECIAL NEEDS

One of the most powerful aspects of a computer operating system is that the input devices (mouse and keyboard) and output information (monitor and speakers) can be configured to support and better help users with special needs. All operating systems (Macintosh, Windows, and Linux) have built-in tools that allow users to reconfigure the way information is received by the computer and then sent back to the user. By changing how the user controls the computer through the use of the mouse, keyboard, or microphone or adjusting the way the monitor displays information can better support users with special needs.

To support the diverse needs of students, teachers should be familiar with the equitable access tools to modify the way the computer receives or sends back information to better support their students with impairments of vision, hearing, physical, and motor skills, as well as learning and literacy. The accessibility tools on an operating system are generally found in the control panel area where other computer configuration tools are located; teachers in today's classrooms should be well versed in how to use these aspects of computer operating systems to support their students with disabilities.

Specifically, Apple includes "Accessibility," which allows users to configure interactive elements within the computer. Accessibility provides support for students with various special needs on all Macintosh, iPhone, iPad, and iPad operating systems. One example is a Voiceover Screen Reader tool for students with limited vision (Apple, 2015). Like the Apple iOS, Linux Distributions Ubuntu, and Linux Mint also label their accessibility tool, "Accessibility." It also allows users to configure the computer environment for those with various special needs. Windows operating systems calls their accessibility tool "Ease of Access" (Microsoft, 2016a).

Apple (2015) provides detailed instructions on how to adapt the Universal Access tools for the Macintosh. Microsoft (2016a) also provides accessibility support. The Lasa Knowledgebase (Lasa Charity UK, Ltd., 2006) provides a good overview of accessibility on Linux-based computers.

TROUBLESHOOTING

Perhaps the best thing one can learn, in terms of computers is to have a good bag of tricks for troubleshooting. Often times, some hardware might have a misconfiguration or it simply doesn't work properly. It is at those times that we often call on the school technology guru. However, the IT personnel often simply go through a list of things that could be wrong, trying things until things work again. It is this trail-and-error method that often provides clues to the problem. Often times if you simply try things, the problem will work itself out.

If, on the other hand, you just can't figure it out and you have no one to call, a quick Internet search may provide the answers. In addition to doing a quick Google search, there are many troubleshooting guides and help websites. For example, the Computer Hope (2016) website provides great basic computer troubleshooting support information.

SCENARIO: ACQUIRING AND INSTALLING OPEN SOURCE SOFTWARE

As you might imagine, many school districts have little funds and keeping technology up to date can be expensive. Let's take a look at Patricia, a tenth-grade teacher, who is designing a unit in which her students will be meeting some outcome of the Social Studies C3-Framework Civics standard, D2.Civ.2.9-12. "Analyze the role of citizens in the U.S. political system, with attention to various theories of democracy, changes in Americans' participation over time, and alternative models from other countries, past and present" (National Council for the Social Studies [NCSS], 2013, p. 32).

In addition, she wants to integrate the Common Core ELA Writing Standards for her grade level. Specifically, she wants them to be able to "Write arguments to support claims in an analysis of substantive topics or texts, using valid reasoning and relevant and sufficient evidence" (Common Core Standards Initiative, 2016, p. 45).

Finally, she also wants to ensure that she can help her students gain better understanding of technology systems that will support their possible future technology needs. Specifically, she wants them to become aware of and are then able to access readily available and open source digital tools when they might not have the financial resources. By doing so, she believes that she is teaching them to locate, download, and install software, thus helping them become more self-sufficient and self-directed learners.

To help her students meet all of these outcomes she decided on a unit in which students will simulate working as campaign aids for the upcoming local election. In teams, they will investigate and choose one of the candidates running for office in their state's upcoming election. Once they've chosen a candidate, they are to design and develop a multimedia brochure that supports their candidate over his or her opponent.

The multimedia brochures must include well-written and accurate information regarding the candidate's position on issues. It must include supporting evidence from credible news articles or other sources that support their candidate's claims. She also wants her students to be able to demonstrate their technology skills, so the brochure must include multimedia, (i.e., images or video of their candidate, audio recordings of speeches and narration) that support their candidate's virtues to support his or her election.

Although Patricia works in a district that has not been able to afford to upgrade their computer lab software for quite some time and might be seen as a disadvantage, she sees an opportunity. Her building technology person has located six older computers that can be moved into her classroom. Although they all work pretty well and have good Internet access, they don't have the software that her students will need to create the multimedia brochures she's requiring. However, she is familiar with online resources and open source software that is available and that can be used or even downloaded and installed on to her newly acquired computers.

Patricia believes that by adding the technology elements to the unit, students will have the opportunity to learn about downloading, installing, and then using these freely available, yet powerful tools. Patricia knows that her students will need a powerful word processor, so she teaches them about the options available but decides to focus on LibreOffice. In addition, she can teach them about the many freely available templates that can be opened in LibreOffice. This decision allows her students to create brochure documents using the various office tools that LibreOffice includes (i.e. word processor, presentation, and drawing program).

Patricia also wants her students to have audio-editing software available. Therefore, she teaches them about Audacity, which is an easy-to-use, yet powerful audio-recording and editing program. With some inexpensive headsets with microphones, her students can record narration to include into their travel brochure.

Patricia knows that her students may also need to have access to a photo-editing program. Therefore, she teaches them how to locate, download, install and use Gimp, a powerful open source image editing program. Patricia's students can use Gimp to organize and edit images they gather for their brochures.

By teaching her students about the various free and open source technology applications, Patricia is integrating technology in such a way as to help them learn where they can locate and install technology tools that will support their learning. In other words, her students become aware of and able to acquire digital age tools that will best suit their needs to support their learning. This gives them the opportunity to demonstrate, and her the opportunity to assess, their understandings and skills of technology operations.

In addition, the multimedia brochure and other organizational materials gives the students the opportunity to meet, and her the opportunity to assess, the outcomes from the social studies and writing standards. By integrating and embedding the technology tools within the lesson, Patricia used the resources she had available to help her students learn about social studies and writing. In addition, she was also teaching them how to use various technology tools. Perhaps more importantly, she was also teaching them how to access the technology resources even with limited financial support. This is a skill that will go far in helping them to be resourceful.

SUMMARY

To integrate technology in ways that will help students have a good understanding of basic technology concepts, it is important for teachers to have a good foundation as well. The primary objective of this chapter is to provide a solid foundation of basic technology foundations and operations. Basic computer information processing and storage operations are compared and contrasted to human brain functions to provide some frame of reference.

In addition, the chapter also discussed the need for classroom teachers to be familiar with and able to configure computers to take advantage of the equitable access tools for students with special needs. These tools are readily available on all computers to help ease the access for all.

The scenario described how a teacher with limited resources but good knowledge can still provide engaging learning opportunities for his or her students. It also provided an overview of some of the software tools that learners can use to engage in working with content, concepts, and skills. Various software applications were discussed from the perspective of how they can be used for learning and not just for classroom management. Think about the software applications as digital tools that can be used by learners to help them demonstrate learning as they construct knowledge, gain understandings of concepts, and practice skills.

REFERENCES

Apple. (2015). Accessibility. iOS. Retrieved from https://www.apple.com/accessibility/ios/.
Atkinson, R. C., and Shiffrin, R. M. (1968). Human memory: A proposed system and its control processes. In R. W. Spence and J. T. Spence (eds.). *The psychology of learning and motivation* (Vol. 2, pp. 89–195). New York: Academic.
Common Core Standards Initiative. (2016). English Language Arts Standards. Retrieved from http://www.corestandards.org/ELA-Literacy/.
Computer Hope. (2016). Basic computer troubleshooting. Retrieved from http://www.computerhope.com/basic.htm.

Canonical Ltd. (2015). About Ubuntu. Retrieved from http://www.ubuntu.com/about/about-ubuntu.

Free Software Foundation, Inc. (2015). *Gimp—The GNU image manipulation program.* Retrieved from http://www.gimp.org/.

Google. (2015). Google Docs: Create and edit documents online, for free. Retrieved from https://www.google.com/docs/about/.

Lasa Charity UK, Ltd. (2006). Lasa Knowledgebase. Retrieved from http://ictknowledgebase.org.uk/linuxaccessibility.

Microsoft. (2016a). Microsoft accessibility. Retrieved from https://www.microsoft.com/enable/

Microsoft. (2016b). OneDrive. Retrieved from https://onedrive.live.com.

Mozilla. (2015a). Firefox web browser. Retrieved from https://www.mozilla.org/en-US/firefox/new/.

Mozilla. (2015b). Mozilla Thunderbird. Retrieved from https://www.mozilla.org/en-US/thunderbird/.

National Council for the Social Studies (NCSS). (2013). *The College, Career, and Civic Life (C3) Framework for Social Studies State Standards: Guidance for Enhancing Rigor of K–12 Civics, Economics, Geography and History.* Silver Spring, MD: Author.

Open Source Initiative. (2015). Welcome to the open source initiative. Retrieved from http://opensource.org/.

Sourceforge.net. (2015). Audacity: Free audio editor and recorder. Retrieved from http://audacity.sourceforge.net/.

The Document Team. (2015). LibreOffice (Version 5.0.4) [Software]. Available from http://www.documentfoundation.org/.

Chapter 5

Global Digital Citizenship

Given the interconnectivity of today's computer networks, students can gather information and resources, download just about any kind of media, and communicate with people around the world. As a classroom teacher you will be responsible for helping your students understand the appropriate use of technologies and digital media. This chapter details various elements of digital citizenship and provides an example of teaching students what it means to be a good digital citizen, indeed a good global digital citizen.

GLOBAL INTERCONNECTION

Technology enables our students to expand their learning environment beyond the confines of the classroom walls to connect with other learners globally. With smartphone applications they can communicate with people across the room or across the oceans. They have access to information, images, animations, audio, and video. Indeed, today's technology tools support our students in many ways, from allowing them to develop and create media-rich digital reports and presentations, as well as communicate and interact with people around the world.

As educators we want students to have access to these powerful tools to enhance their learning opportunities, whether it be through access to vast information and resources or communicating with people of other cultures. We want students to become part of and behave as good citizens of this global digital society, but with these opportunities, comes great responsibilities.

Inappropriate use of technology is a grave concern. To combat cyberbullying, most states in the United States now have laws and legislation to help solve this serious issue. Most schools or districts require students to sign an "appropriate use" policy, which outlines the dos and don'ts of using technology while at school. Many schools limit or restrict some technology use by students, such as a no cell phone policy, which restricts any cell phone use in school.

Szoka and Thierer (2009) believe that limiting access to technology, such as cell phones, limits learning opportunities and suggest that education is preferable to restrictive policies and legislation. Instead of limiting a student's access to digital tools educators should focus teaching students to understand appropriate behavior and making good choices when they use technology.

Students will be using their cell phones and other technologies outside of school. Therefore, it is important to teach students appropriate and socially responsible technology use, both in and outside of school. In other words, the task should be teaching them what it means to be good digital citizens within the digital society within which we all now belong.

DIGITAL CITIZENSHIP

Ribble (2015) outlines nine themes of digital citizenship that begins in kindergarten with three topics: Respect, Educate, and Protect. The nine themes are digital access, digital commerce, digital communication, digital literacy, digital etiquette, digital law, digital rights and responsibilities, digital health and wellness, and digital security. One way of thinking about teaching these concepts is to group them into teachable elements.

Digital Literacy

Teaching students to be good digital citizens should start with digital literacy. Becoming literate and purposeful users of technology is one of the foundations that will serve them well. However, it is also important for students to know that because of the constant changes in technology, digital literacy doesn't end; they need to be lifelong learners.

Specifically, good digital citizens need to be aware that there are a great deal of new technologies becoming available continually and that one needs to keep honing and helping others hone their technology skills. However, digital literacy is not just about learning new technologies. Although these digital tools provide great opportunities, they also have inherent dangers.

Students need to become aware of the nature and responsibilities of free speech and being able to balance this double-edged sword when communicating electronically. For example, when communicating electronically it could be easy to forget that there is a human being at the end of every communication and that appropriate etiquette should always be sought and taught when digitally interacting with others.

Social media tools can easily be used for harm when students lack care in their communication. Traditional or cyberbullying can both be harmful for targeted children (Modecki, Minchin, Harbaugh, Guerra, and Runions, 2014). Teaching students to understand the importance of practicing compassion and tolerance when using electronic communication tools is vital in order for them to become good digital citizens.

Students also need to become familiar with healthy habits of ergonomics for physical and intellectual well-being by learning about possible harm from the technological world we now live in. In particular, they should become aware of and keep up to date on security issues for personal identity safety. It is vital for them to understand that their personal information should never be made readily available online. In addition to personal safety, students should also become familiar with and practice protecting ones data and equipment from viral attacks and electronic malfunctions by following good file backup practices.

Digital Commerce and Law

We live in a world of digital commerce where goods and services are bought and sold daily. Although this aspect of today's life might seem normal to many, it hasn't been too many years since this trend has occurred. Because lawmaking is much slower than technology developments, some of the laws and regulations that govern digital commerce are still being written. Students need to become aware of issues that will impact their lives. For example, the electronic marketplace operates from many different nations. Foreign laws and regulations often vary and may be in conflict with those of which one may be aware.

Over the past decade advances in technology have brought copyright issues to the forefront as many artists now distribute their works via the Internet. A good example is iTunes (Apple, 2015). Students need to understand, comply with, and teach others respect for and appropriate use of digital media, including music, art, and words. In addition, good digital citizens do no harm to others' work or invade privacy. They need to understand that illegally downloading music, videos, or images is copyright infringement.

There are, however, times when what may look like copyright infringement is really "fair use." In addition, there are some "works" that are not limited by copyright, which means that you can freely download and use, and it is not considered to be piracy. There are many open source or general-public licensed software that are freely available to download and install. This can cause a bit of confusion, and copyright laws can be a bit tricky for some teachers. Luckily, there are many resources to help teachers and their students learn the specifics of copyright laws.

Ethics

Students are often required to research information and then write up a report to demonstrate what they've learned. Certainly, search engines and the Internet make this task much easier and, in a sense, more powerful because of the vast amount of information and resources at a student's finger tips. Because of the ease of copy and pasting text from a Web site to one's paper, it is easy to fall prey to plagiarism. Without a good understanding of appropriate use of materials and resources and citing sources properly, many students have plagiarized.

For students to be ethical researchers and writers, it is vital for them to respect another's original work. Perhaps one of the best resources to help students learn good citation habits is Purdue's Online Writing Lab (Purdue OWL, 2016), a Web site that outlines APA, MLA, and other writing styles.

Copyright and Fair Use

Copyright laws protect authors' literary, dramatic, musical, artistic, and other creative works from other people profiting from the author's original work. However, copyright laws vary between countries, which becomes important when thinking about being a global digital citizen. For example, many countries have ratified the Berne Convention treaty that protects artistic works; other countries have not, some disregarding copyright protection altogether (World Intellectual Property Organization, 2015).

One of the best resources available that can provide some quick answers to questions regarding U.S. Copyright is the FAQs on copyright.gov (Copyright Law Office, 2015) Web site. U.S. Copyright begins to protect an original work, "the moment it is created and fixed in a tangible form that it is perceptible either directly or with the aid of a machine or device" (para. 4). In other words, an author is not required to register their work with the U.S. Copyright office to be copyright protected, but it is recommended.

Therefore, if a student comes across an image they want to use, unless it states otherwise, it is copyrighted. If a student creates an original work it could be copyright protected, but it depends on the state in which you're teaching. Some states have regulations regarding minors doing business dealings that involve copyright.

Although it may seem that because every work of art is copyrighted the moment it's posted online, the best approach to helping students become good digital citizens is to not allow them to download any digital media. However, there is an element of copyright law that permits the use of copyrighted material without it being a copyright infringement. "Fair use" limits exclusive rights for copyrighted material and original works can be used without breaking the law.

According to the U.S. Copyright Law Office (2015), the factors that determine fair use of original copyrighted material include "a) the purpose and character of the use, including whether such use is of a commercial nature or is for nonprofit educational purposes, b) the nature of the copyrighted work, c) the amount and substantiality of the portion used in relation to the copyrighted work as a whole; and d) the effect of the use upon the potential market for or value of the copyrighted work" (para. 107).

In other words, teachers and students can use copyrighted material if it falls under fair use. This means that for many classroom activities, depending on the copyrighted material, and that provided the work (that include copyrighted digital media) is not published, is not going to be sold, and that the work doesn't include a substantial amount of the copyrighted whole, it will fall under the fair use policy.

Open Source and General Public License

Although most software and digital media is copyrighted, there are many resources that are open to the public and freely available. The General Public License movement and Open Source Initiative (2015) are resources of which all classroom teachers should be fully aware. By teaching and modeling the use the use of these freely available resources teachers will be helping their students become more digitally literate and better able to resist the temptation of becoming software pirates by alleviating need for the illegal acquisition of software.

The Foundations of the General Public License v.3 (Free Software Foundation, Inc., 2014) states: "Nobody should be restricted by the software they use. There are four freedoms that every user should have: a) the freedom to use the software for any purpose, b) the freedom to change the software to suit your needs, c) the freedom to share the software with your friends and neighbors, and d) the freedom to share the changes you make. When a program offers users all of these freedoms, we call it free software" (para 2).

Open source software includes operating systems, productivity tools, and various other applications that can be downloaded for free. In addition, there are many other free software titles available for educators. A great resource is opensource.com (2015), which reviewed open source school management software programs for teachers and students.

Digital Access

Good digital citizens need to be aware that not all have the same access to technology tools and resources and that equitable access is a goal to which a good digital citizen is committed. There are socioeconomic and political barriers that might limit digital access both here in the United States and globally. Certainly, if a student doesn't have access to technology, whether it be the computer or the Internet, they are limited in their access. Additionally, if digital access is limited because of censorship, whether it is for safety or political reasons, access is then not equitable to those who do not have those limitations.

Other students may not have equitable access but not because of the lack of computers at home or school or censorship. Some students have limited access because they have special needs that limit their digital access because of a physical, visual, hearing, or other impairment. Classroom teachers should be aware that any limiting factor to digital access is inequitable access. Helping students to become good digital citizens includes teaching them how they might help others access technology.

Teachers should become familiar with the *equitable access* tools that are built into all computer operating systems to support various special needs users. There are several ways to change the configuration of the computer to enhance the access for a variety of impairments, such as vision, hearing, physical, and motor skills, as well as learning and literacy. In addition, there are software applications that can be installed to further support those with special needs. For example, those with vision loss can purchase commercial screen readers for Windows-based computers, such as Job Access with Speech (Freedom Scientific, Inc., 2015).

Teaching students to be good digital citizens means that they should become aware of social inequities and how these constraints limit access, thus helping students understand and gain a broader perspective and expand their global awareness. Good digital citizens are aware that limitations to digital access can be economic or political in nature, but it can also be the result of one's special needs (i.e., ability to see, hear, and manipulate the technologies). Indeed, a good digital citizen is aware of and works toward the goal of equitable access, regardless of any limitations.

GLOBAL DIGITAL CITIZENSHIP

Crawford and Kirby (2008) describe how technology can support global education, which helps students see themselves as global citizens. "The infusion of global education in K–12 schooling thought the appropriate and effective use of various technologies is essential. By incorporating numerous technologies in authentic and meaningful ways in social studies teaching and learning, as supported by the technological pedagogical content knowledge (TPCK) framework, teachers can foster students' understandings about the interrelationships of peoples worldwide, thereby preparing students to think as global citizens" (p. 71).

Picardo (2012) discusses the opportunities for character-building experiences in study abroad programs. "Global awareness and international collaboration during the formative years results in more rounded individuals, encouraging our pupils to see things from different perspectives and helping them to make informed decisions, acquiring transferable skills that will be useful to them and will remain with them for life" (para. 10).

Although not the same experience as a study abroad program, using technologies such as Twitter (2015) and Skype (2014), students can connect with others internationally. Setting up international collaborations and ePals (2015) can offer students the opportunity to interact with others of differing cultures. For example, students may quickly discover that they have more or perhaps less access to technology resources and tools than their international peers. This type of activity may greatly enhance the opportunity for students to discuss and reflect on the first theme of digital citizenship, digital access, especially if there is no equitable access for all.

This type of international collaboration may increase opportunities to discuss and reflect on other digital citizenship themes, such as *digital commerce, digital law*, and *digital security*. The more global experience of an international collaboration can provide a contextual foundation to discuss, reflect, and practice *digital etiquette* given the possible cross cultural differences that may influence the interaction, perhaps positively, perhaps negatively.

With social media, electronic messaging, and Internet-based applications students can communicate in a more global environment. Integrating technology on a global scale can help students gain a better understanding of other cultures as they become aware of cultural differences. Teaching students appropriate ways of communicating via the digital tools can help them gain a more global perspective of greater tolerance and cultural understanding. As students gain an expanded global awareness they will learn about their *digital rights and responsibilities* as global digital citizens within this global community.

SCENARIO: FOSTERING GLOBAL DIGITAL CITIZENSHIP

Geraldo is a tenth-grade social studies teacher who teaches in a school district that, despite having a well-defined "appropriate technology use policy" that all students must sign, has been having some events of cyberbullying. The administration decided to ask teachers to prepare and teach a unit that will help students gain a better understanding of what that means.

Geraldo has read that there are a lot of similarities between traditional bullying and cyberbullying, but that social media tools permit students to communicate with others far beyond their local classrooms and in a much more personal manner. He knows that if students lack compassion or tolerance for others, they can easily use these tools for harm.

Geraldo decides that, although cyberbullying has been the problem, it would be best to design a unit that will include all aspects of global digital citizenship. By doing so, he can address appropriate use of social media but within the context of global digital citizenship. He believes that doing so will help alleviate any unwanted attention on those who might be bullied.

Wanting his students to become good digital citizens he believes that his objectives for this unit should include items from the ISTE Student Technology Standard on Digital Literacy (2015): "Students understand human, cultural, and societal issues related to technology and practice legal and ethical behavior." He decides he will focus on four topics:

- Safe, ethical, and legal use of technology
- Socially responsible digital use
- Equitable access of technology
- Global awareness and cultural understanding

Geraldo decides that to help them understand these four topics he will use a collaborative learning technique called *jigsaw*. In this jigsaw unit students will join home teams of four (and some with five for some of his classes). Each student in each home team will select one of the four topics (teams of five will split safe, ethical, and legal use) and investigate what that means.

To help them do that, students will join a like-topic group (i.e., all "socially responsible digital use" students will work together) will work together to gather information on what that topic means. Each of the like-topic groups will use Google Slides (2015) to create a presentation that details their topic and provides specific examples of appropriate use and inappropriate use for that topic. Once they complete their presentations, students will rejoin their home team and take turns using their topic presentation to teach their teammates about their individual topic.

Students will then rejoin their like-topic group and create a scenario that is a plausible real-life situation in which students are not being good digital citizens with respect to that topic. In addition, the scenario must include the use of social media in some fashion. Once the scenarios are created, the students then take turns acting out their scenario in front of the class. Once completed, Geraldo will have the class discuss the situation that was acted out in terms of what behavior was inappropriate and how it could have been alleviated or eliminated.

In thinking about how he will assess his students on this unit, Geraldo decides that each student in the like-topic group will create an individual presentation where they must describe how being a good digital citizen in their topic might impact society, both on a global and local scale. In addition, he defines specific criteria for like-topic group presentations.

For "safe, ethical, and legal use of technology," students must include detailed information in terms of safety and security. Their presentation must also include detailed information on ethical use, in terms of plagiarism, and information on legal use, in terms of copyright and piracy.

For "socially responsible" use, the presentation must include detailed information on appropriate use of social media (i.e., cyberbullying and privacy).

For "equitable access," the presentation must include detailed information on various ways others might be limited in technology access (i.e., economic, geopolitical, physical, and cognitive).

For "global awareness and cultural understanding," the presentations must include detailed information on cultural insensitivity, compassion, and tolerance.

As students teach their home teams their topics, Geraldo plans on observing the students, which will serve as his formative assessment. Geraldo's observations of the students as they act out their scenarios and the subsequent discussions will serve as an additional formative assessment of the unit.

To provide a summative assessment beyond the topic slide presentations, Geraldo will require each student to read a scenario of a fictitious event where two students use social media to cyberbully another student. Each student will be assessed on their ability to identify the inappropriate behavior, how the bullied student might feel, and what they might do to help alleviate the situation.

SUMMARY

Technology has made the world a much smaller place and our students now have instant access to information, digital media, and individuals across the globe. Although today's students may be quite familiar using these tools, they might not understand the impact of inappropriate use. Given this new global society, it is vital that we teach our students what it means to be a good digital citizen.

This chapter has defined digital citizen using Ribble's (2015) nine themes of digital citizenship. The notion of global digital citizenship requires students to become more globally aware with better understandings of cultural differences that support cross cultural interactions. Being aware of and practicing these tenets within the global digital society is being a good global digital citizen.

Classroom teachers are expected to help their students understand the appropriate use of technology in all phases of learning. Students should be aware of and practice safe and secure technology use. Digitally literacy includes an awareness of digital commerce, obeying digital laws, and practicing appropriate use of technology for communication, publishing, and productivity. It's important for them to understand their digital rights and responsibilities, which include the right to equitable digital access and the responsibility to be aware of and to try to help those who might have limited or no access.

The scenario for this chapter provided an example of how a teacher might address cyberbullying, a growing problem, by teaching the broader spectrum of global digital citizenship. It included some details of using a collaborative teaching method, jigsaw, which provides support of group interdependence but also provides for individual accountability.

It is important to understand that teaching students good digital citizenship habits, indeed, habits of a good global digital citizen provides a foundation for the appropriate use of technology throughout their lives.

REFERENCES

Apple. (2015). Apple. Retrieved from https://www.apple.com.
Copyright Law Office. (2015). Copyright Law: Chapter 1. Retrieved from http://www.copyright.gov/title17/92chap1.html#107.
Crawford, E. O., and Kirby, M. M. (2008). Fostering students' global awareness: Technology applications in social studies teaching and learning. *Journal of Curriculum and Instruction,* (1), 5673.
ePals. (2015). Where learners connect. Retrieved fromhttp://www.epals.com/.
Free Software Foundation, Inc. (2014). *A Quick Guide to GPLv3—GNU Project.* Retrieved from http://www.gnu.org/licenses/quick-guide-gplv3.html.
Freedom Scientific, Inc. (2015). JAWS screen reader—Best in class. Retrieved fromhttp://www.freedomscientific.com/Products/Blindness/JAWS.
International Society for Technology in Education (ISTE). (2015). Standards*S for Students. Retrieved from http://www.iste.org/standards/standards-for-students.
Modecki, K. L., Minchin, J., Harbaugh, A. G., Guerra, N. G., and Runions, K. C. (2014). Bullying prevalence across contexts: A meta-analysis measuring cyber and traditional bullying. *Journal of Adolescent Health,* 55(5), 602–611.
Opensource.com. (2015). A review of open source software programs for school management. Reviewed fromhttp://opensource.com/life/13/1/three-open-source-school-management-software-programs-teachers-and-student.
Open Source Initiative. (2015). Welcome to the open source initiative. Retrieved from http://opensource.org/.
Picardo, J. (2012). Why students need global awareness and understandings of other cultures. Retrieved from http://www.theguardian.com/teachernetwork/2012/sep/25/studentsglobalawarenessothercultures.
Purdue Online Writing Lab (OWL). (2016). Retrieved fromhttps://owl.english.purdue.edu/.
Ribble, M. (2015). Nine elements. Retrieved from http://www.digitalcitizenship.net/Nine_Elements.html.
Skype. (2015). Skype. Retrieved from http://www.skype.com.
Szoka, B. M., and Thierer, A. D. (2009). Cyberbullying legislation: Why education is preferable to regulation. *Progress & Freedom Foundation Progress on Point Paper, 16*(12).
Twitter.com (2015). Retrieved from https://twitter.com

World Intellectual Property Organization. (2015). Berne Convention for the Protection of Literary and Artistic Works. Retrieved from http://www.wipo.int/treaties/en/ip/berne/.

Chapter 6

Communication and Collaboration

With today's digital communication tools, it is possible for students to work collaboratively, thus expanding their ability to support and enhance their learning and contribute to the learning of others. This chapter will discuss specific digital communication and collaboration tools that support student learning in a variety of ways. By learning how to use these digital communication tools, students have an opportunity to gain a better understanding of how to collaborate with peers, experts, and others to share ideas, contribute to team projects to create shared original works, and solve problems.

DIGITAL COMMUNICATION AND COLLABORATION TOOLS

With only an Internet connection and a browser, students have been able to engage with other students across vast distances using a variety of communication tools, such as e-mail, discussion boards, chat, and instant messaging. Although these text-based tools have provided opportunities for students to communicate, interact, and even collaborate, there are new digital communication and collaboration tools being developed daily.

Audio- and video-conferencing tools allow students to not only communicate but also to co-edit a document at the same time. Crenzel and Nojima (2006) quote *Claire*, who was age eight at the time, to explain why she prefers the aspect of interactive communication. "The TV is just there, and you just sit and watch and do nothing. I just can't stand to do nothing. Messenger is a lot better: you talk and someone talks back to you, it's a lot more fun" (p. 6). Now a decade later consider what *Claire* at age eighteen might think about today's free video-conferencing tools such as Skype (2015) or Google Hangouts (2015d).

It is important to remember, however, that students have greater responsibilities when using these powerful communication tools and students need to understand and practice good global digital citizenship. It is important for students to use etiquette when interacting with others regardless of where they may be located. Digital safety and security must also be considered by both teachers and parents. There are tools that can help secure these interactive environments, such as classroom-safe applications and Web sites of which one should become aware.

Digital communication tools, particularly mobile phones, have changed the way we communicate and have become important (Henley, 2010). They are used for just about every kind of communication: voice, textual, and visual. Because of these tools, communication has changed, and in many ways, it has lost some detail or richness, but in others it has gained details.

Given the different ways some of these tools are used, many fall into the category of *social media* and are designed to allow people to share and exchange elements of their lives (i.e., comments, ideas, photos, and videos). Think about how differently one communicates using text, Twitter (2015), Instagram (2015), e-mail, a discussion board, or a forum. Indeed, Instagram isn't written communication, rather it is visual communication.

Synchronous and Asynchronous Tools

Today's digital tools have changed how we communicate; educators and researchers are rethinking the notion of literacy and teaching (Walsh, 2008; Sweeny, 2010; Bogard and McMackin, 2012). Some asynchronous communication tools provide some element of time for reflective writing, whereas others are synchronous and happen at the same time. Even though texting is asynchronous, think about how fast one receives and then replies to a message. Because communicating via text can be so swift and many digital devices have limited keyboards for typing, users often use abbreviations (e.g., LOL, BFF, IMHO, BTW, etc.).

Using synchronous tools for a class or group discussion requires that users interact in real time. Having to respond or reply quickly requires students to reply with their immediate thoughts. However, because they are immediate, there may be little reflection. Also, a student's keyboarding skills may impact his or her ability to engage in a swiftly moving discussion, thus leaving them out of the conversation.

Texting or SMS Clicker Student Response Systems can also be used for instant assessment of student understanding. Although not synchronous, teachers can check quickly for their students' general understandings of concepts. Teachers can also take instant polls by having students use clickers to respond to questions, which then are immediately displayed as a pie chart that graphically displays the breakdown of the classes' opinion on a topic.

Although these can be powerful tools, Student Response Systems can be expensive.

E-mail is used by many classroom teachers for a variety of communication tasks with students and their parents to send out announcements, newsletters, or individual communiques. Teachers can also have their students use e-mail as a way to learn good writing skills by having them to practice formal writing. Rather than allowing students to sloppily write down their thoughts or ideas in an e-mail, a teacher can have students collect their thoughts, compose their ideas, and refine their writing in a word processor to practice good sentence structure, grammar, spelling, and punctuation.

Blogs (web log) allow students to journal and publish their thoughts or comments to their own personal blog. Blogs can be configured to be private, available to only those invited, or to the world (Google, 2015a). Having students create their own blog provides opportunities to share their thoughts or understandings of or reflections on a topic. Lacina and Griffith (2012) describe fourth-grade students using their blogs to support reading instruction, specifically the reading strategy of prediction. After the teacher reads the first half of a book, she then asks the students to write their predictions of what will happen next.

Wikis are yet another tool that provides for online communication and collaboration; Wikipedia (2015) is the most famous wiki. In addition to open source wiki applications that can be set up on a school server for teachers and students, Google Sites (2015c) permits users to set up free private, shared, or open to the public Web sites where students can co-author Web pages, have discussion, and post files. By co-authoring a publication in this manner students contribute to their group's or team's effort to produce an original work.

Learning Management Systems

BlackBoard (2015), or the open source, Moodle (2015), are good examples of learning management systems (LMS). These tools provide an online learning area for content, as well as a variety of communication and collaboration digital tools together in a private and safe learning environment. They also include elements to provide for a host of other tools, such as information presentation, grade book, assignment drop box, and learner tracking.

Although many school districts provide an LMS to support pre-K–12 classroom teachers, there are other tools that teachers can access for free. Edmodo (2015) is a similar application for all grade levels. Once teachers create an Edmodo account, they can then create a class environment in which they can post assignments, resources, and practice items. One of the powerful elements of an Edmodo account is that lesson plans can also be embedded, which are directly aligned to specific Common Core Standards of both English–Language Arts and Mathematics.

Social Media Tools

Twitter, a popular social media tool, allows users to post messages that include a maximum of 140 characters and up to four images in one *tweet*. Because of the limited amount of a message, Twitter could be considered a microblogging tool and used as a way to share, present, or announce information. Teachers might have their students follow their Twitter account to provide announcements. Or as Borau, Ullrich, Feng, and Shen (2009) describe, teachers can use Twitter for learners of English as a way to help them practice and enhance their communicative and cultural competence.

Instagram, another social media tool, allows users to share elements of their lives through photos and can provide direct feeds to their Facebook account. Blair and Serafini (2014) describe integrating a variety of social media tools into the classroom. They suggest having students create a video book review and posting it to their Instagram account. English-language learners can practice language skills by creating photo essays on specific topics or themes, such as illustrating science or other academic projects.

Facebook is probably the best-known social media tool, but integrating it into a classroom requires some forethought and care. Teachers posting personal beliefs and stories can impact student motivation and affective learning and classroom climate because students feel that it is a bit of an invasion into their out-of-school lives (Mazer, Murphy and Simonds, 2007; Munoz and Towner, 2009) However, Hull (2014) described how a high school teacher created a class Facebook page, which was more about the class than the teacher, and it helped create a sense of community and kept high school students informed.

WEB 2.0: LEARNER-GENERATED CONTENT

Web 2.0 are sites where the users generate the content. For example, the Meredith Corporation's Recipe.com (2015) is a Web 2.0 site, which might better be called a *Web service* because users create accounts and then post their recipes to share with others. Facebook is probably the most well known of all Web 2.0 sites because it provides the venue, but all of the users create the content with their profile and posts.

Web 2.0 Classroom Examples

There are many Web 2.0 resources for both elementary and secondary classroom teachers. One good example of a safe and free resource is Diigo (2015), a website where users can create and share bookmarks of good Web sites. After creating a free account, students can use these to organize their research findings. Because Diigo is a social bookmarking tool, they can also search out topics that others have "tagged." In addition, students can highlight text directly on any Web page that they've bookmarked.

Another popular example, is Glogster (2015). Students access the Web site using computers or tablets and create *Glogs*, which are electronic posters on teacher-assigned topics using predesigned graphics or images from the Web. Teachers can create a class account, which provides a safe location for their class to create and share their Glogs.

Collaborative Productivity Tools

Online productivity tools are designed to support collaboration in which students can work at the same time on a shared document. Google Docs (Google, 2015b) permits sharing, thus allowing collaboration and co-authoring. Microsoft OneDrive Live (2015) also provides free use of the online suite of productivity tools, which allows for sharing and co-editing of documents, spreadsheets, slide shows, and other files. Using these tools permits co-authoring for students who are located anywhere around the globe that have Internet access. This provides a good opportunity for students to work with others regardless of their location.

USING DIGITAL COMMUNICATION AND COLLABORATION TOOLS SAFELY

Students are able to use a search engine to access just about any kind of content, which depending on grade level can become a safety issue. Monitoring students using these tools is important because some sites are censored, which limits how search engines and other communication and collaboration tools might function.

In addition to being able to use a search engine to access just about any kind of content, students can also connect with others using a variety of powerful communication and collaboration tools and are not limited to the text-based communication and collaboration systems. They can also use Internet conferencing systems, such as Skype® and Elluminate® that provide synchronous audio and video communication with an inexpensive headset and microphone.

Some believe that students using a variety of these tools to create their own personal learning environment provides greater learner control because students are required to organize and use a variety of digital communication and collaboration tools to create their own personal learning environment (Attwell, 2007). Because students need to organize the various communication and collaboration tools to best suit their learning needs, it requires them to be more aware of how to identify and better use resources.

A confined learning management system could be considered safer because all of the communication and collaboration happens within the enclosed system. However, when students create their own personal learning environment using Web 2.0 and other open communication and collaboration tools, it provides greater opportunities for learning as they assemble, organize, and interact with others using various open communication and collaboration tools.

Although permitting students to use more open communication and collaboration tools might provide greater opportunities for them to interact and learn on a more global scale, it brings up safety issues. Some schools or districts require teachers to use specific tools or learning systems, such as Blackboard. Others may have few or no restrictions on how students use some of the tools discussed. Another option that many school districts are taking is subscribing to the Google Classroom (Google, 2016), which includes Google Docs, Gmail, and Google Calendar in a free safe and secure web-based environment.

SCENARIO: WEB 2.0 IN LEARNING–POPULATION PROBLEM

Judith and Mark are eighth-grade teachers at one of middle schools within their district and often worked together to align the district's science curriculum with the Next Generation Science Standard HS-ESS3-4 Earth and Human Activity (Achieve, 2015) and Common Core ELA/Literacy Standards WHST 6-8 for science writing (Common Core State Standards Initiative, 2015).They decided to develop a unit in which their students would investigate Human Activity, which would give them the opportunity to "Construct an argument supported by evidence for how increases in human population and per-capita consumption of natural resources impact Earth's systems"

As they looked more deeply into the NGSS HS-ESS3-4, they realized that there were connections to the CC-ELA performance indicators provided and that they believed that they could then enhance their unit by adding them. To help their students meet the performance indicators for this standard of Earth and Human Activity, the unit engaged the students in the process of scientific inquiry.

Additionally, students will use communication and collaboration tools to help collect and analyze data with other science students across the country, thus supporting their students in becoming part of a larger science learning community. Finally, to facilitate the collaboration between the classes, Judith and Mark had requested from their administration that their science classes be held at the same time, so sometimes they could meet as an entire group and perhaps mix their students between the classes. Although this was tricky, their administration figured out a way for this to happen because it was essential for the success of this unit.

The classes met together and using a SMART Board® to project a computer cognitive mapping software, Mark and Judith introduce the unit by posing the question to their classes. "How does population growth in the United States impact environmental quality and natural resources?" During the following discussion, several things were decided. First, they needed to define *environmental quality*. Second, they needed to figure out how they would get information on *population growth* and *natural resources*.

Mark and Judith helped guide the discussion and suggested the U.S. Census Bureau Web site (U.S. Department of Commerce, 2015) could provide information on population growth and the U.S. Environmental Protection Agency (2015) Web site could help define and provide information on the environment, which is defined as air, water, land, and quality, as level of pollutants.

Mark then suggested that they might also be able to get help from other students living in other states by creating an online survey using Google Forms (Google, 2015e). As a member of the ePals (Cricket Media, Inc. 2015) learning community, teachers often asked other members of the community to help with their classroom projects. Mark didn't think it would be too difficult to get students in other states to fill out the Google survey asking them to submit information they had on the quality of their air and water in their states.

Mark and Judith took turns demonstrating to each of the classes' two online resources and digital tools that would be used for the project. Mark demonstrated the Google Sites (2015s) area that he had set up for the project. He instructed the students that this was a free resource provided by Google, but he had protected the site so only those working on the project would have access. Each team would be given two pages on the site, where they could enter information that they found about their particular states. Google Sites serves as a formative assessment of the project progress and individual student engagement.

One of the pages is the survey, which would be developed in Google Forms. As participants submit their surveys, data are entered into a Google Sheets spreadsheet file, which will serve as the project database. Once data is available in the spreadsheet, students can run various statistical analysis to help them interpret the results. In addition to gathering information, it can also display information, such as the Diigo Web site resources.

Judith demonstrated Diigo (Diigo, 2015) that they were to use for the project. She had created a class account and demonstrated how they could create and organize a bookmark list of Web site resources they would find. Each student who created a bookmark was to also add a comment, which described its qualities and reference information regarding the site, including information on the individual or agency responsible for the information, the date that the information was found, and descriptions of any other helpful details of what might be found at the site.

She told them that this was a great tool because they could annotate and highlight items within the bookmarked pages, which would allow them to begin to organize and prioritize the information and resources they were collecting. In addition, Judith suggested that they think about a tagging scheme so that the bookmarks could be organized by topics when shared. The Diigo bookmarks served as a formative assessment to check on overall project progress and individual engagement.

Judith and Mark organized the class into two teams, where one team would work on organizing the survey and a database to collect the information once it was submitted. The survey and database team would also be responsible for finding students in other states who would be willing to fill out the surveys. In developing the survey, Mark suggested that it be in two different parts: (a) getting information on what natural resources each state was known for and the status of those resources, and (b) getting information about each state's air and water quality.

The other team would work on state population data and developing the project Google Site. The state population and Web site resource team would be responsible for getting population growth data, which would then be entered into the research database. In addition, this team would be responsible for locating and making Diigo Web site resources to be available for any participant in the investigation; either in Mark or Judith's classes or those students in other states who might use the resources to help them answer the questions on the survey.

Students were then put into groups of three within their respective classes and asked to look at the "aggregate" data, or average the data, rather than any one city or state for their conclusions. As they looked at these data in the Google Forms responses spreadsheet, they were to look for changes in population, quality of air and water or natural resources, and draw some conclusions on what they thought the correlation data analysis meant. In addition, they could select a particular city or state as an example, to demonstrate their point.

Each team worked collaboratively to create and present a final PowerPoint presentation to include slides with bulleted lists, including a title slide; overview of project slide; process slide; findings and data analysis slides (i.e., changes in population, air and water quality, and natural resources); conclusion slides that state the impact to the appearance, composition, and structure of Earth's systems based on population growth; and make predictions of future populations and environmental quality in ten, twenty-five, and fifty years. The presentations served as a summative assessment based on the quality and depth of information.

Each student was then responsible for writing up a final report using Google Docs, which included similar criteria as the team presentation, but including more specific written details expected. They could use the team's final presentation as a resource and ask other team members for clarification, should they have questions. However, each individual student's final report served as the individual summative assessment using the Next Generation Science Standard HS-ESS3-4 Earth and Human Activity and Common Core ELA/Literacy Standards for science writing.

SUMMARY

The purpose of this chapter is to provide readers with a solid foundation of digital communication and collaboration tools that can be used to integrate into classroom instruction in ways that are safe and powerful. Beginning with an overview of synchronous and asynchronous communication tools, the discussion moved to more complex synchronous video conferencing and Web 2.0 tools and digital collaboration tools in which learners can create the content as they create digital artifacts that demonstrate their learning.

Although integrating these digital communication and collaboration tools can be powerful methods to enhance your students' learning, it is also important that teachers have a good understanding of safety measures. Although communicating and collaborating with other learners and experts can provide more real-life learning experiences, there can also be dangers because students will be in direct contact with others outside of your classroom, perhaps state, or even country.

Integrating digital tools such as today's social media, which is frequented by anyone, might be exciting and cool, but it must be done with care. Remember that the notion of being and modeling good digital citizenship will provide a good example for appropriate use of these powerful tools.

REFERENCES

Achieve, Inc. (2015). Next Generation Science Standards: For states, by states. (NGSS). *HS-ESS3-4: Earth and human activity*. Retrieved from http://www.nextgenscience.org/hsess3-earth-human-activity.

Attwell, G. (2007). Personal learning environments—the future of eLearning? *eLearning papers*, 2(1), 1–8.

BlackBoard Inc. (2015). Retrieved from http://www.blackboard.com/.

Blair, R., and Serafini, T. M. (2014). Integration of education: Using social media networks to engage students. *Systemics, Cybernetics and Informatics*, 12(6), 23–31.

Bogard, J. M., and McMackin, M. C. (2012). Combining traditional and new literacies in a 21st-century writing workshop. *The Reading Teacher*, 65(5), 313–323.

Borau, K., Ullrich, C., Feng, J., and Shen, R. (2009). Microblogging for language learning: Using twitter to train communicative and cultural competence. In M. Spaniol, Q. Li, R.

Klamma, and R. W. H. Lau (eds.). *Advances in Web Based Learning–ICWL 2009* (pp. 78–87). Berlin, Germany: Springer.
Common Core State Standards Initiative. (2015). Preparing America's students for college and career. English Language Arts Standards. Retrieved from http://www.corestandards.org/ELA-Literacy/WHST/6-8/.
Crenzel, S. R., and Nojima, B. L. (2006). Children and instant messaging. *Ergonomics 4 Children*.
Cricket Media, Inc. (2015). ePals: Where learners connect. Retrieved from http://www.epals.com/.
Diigo, Inc. (2015). Better reading and researching with annotations, highlighter, sticky notes, archiving, bookmarking and more. Retrieved from https://www.diigo.com/.
Edmodo. (2015). Edmodo.com: Connect with students and parents in your paperless classroom. Retrieved from https://www.edmodo.com/.
Glogster EDU. (2015). Create and explore educational content online. Retrieved from http://edu.glogster.com.
Google. (2015a). Blogger. Retrieved from https://www.blogger.com/.
Google. (2015b). Google Docs. Retrieved from https://www.google.com/docs/about/.
Google. (2015c). Google sites. Retrieved from https://apps.google.com/intx/en_us/products/sites/.
Google. (2015d). Google hangouts. Retrieved from:https://plus.google.com/hangouts.
Google (2015e) Google Forms. Retrieved from https://www.google.com/forms/about.
Google. (2016). Google classroom help. Retrieved from https://support.google.com/edu/classroom/answer/6020279?hl=en.
Henley, J. (2010). Teenagers and technology: "I'd rather give up my kidney than my phone." *The Guardian*. Retrieved from http://www.appohigh.org/ourpages/auto/2013/4/19/54668350/Teenagers%20and%20technology.docx.
Hull, K. (2014). Using Facebook in the classroom. *International Journal of Social Media and Interactive Learning Environments*, 2(1), 60–69.
Instagram.com. (2015). Retrieved from:https://instagram.com/.
Lacina, J., and Griffith, R. (2012). Blogging as a means of crafting writing. *The Reading Teacher*, 66(4), 316–320.
Mazer, J. P., Murphy, R. E., and Simonds, C. J. (2007). I'll see you on "Facebook": The effects of computer-mediated teacher self-disclosure on student motivation, affective learning, and classroom climate. *Communication Education*, 56(1), 1–17.
Meredith Corporation. (2015). Recipe.com: Quick recipes, easy meal ideas. Retrieved from http://recipe.com
Microsoft OneDrive Live. (2015). Word, Excel, and PowerPoint on the Web. Retrieved from https://office.live.com/start/default.aspx.
Moodle. (2015). Open-source learning platform. Retrieved from https://moodle.org/.
Munoz, C., and Towner, T. (2009, March). Opening Facebook: How to use Facebook in the college classroom. In *Society for information technology and teacher education international conference*, 1, 2623–2627.
Skype.com. (2015). Free calls to friends and family. Retrieved from http://www.skype.com/en/.
Sweeny, S. M. (2010). Writing for the instant messaging and text messaging generation: Using new literacies to support writing instruction. *Journal of Adolescent and Adult Literacy*, 54(2), 121–130.
Twitter.com. (2015). Retrieved from https://twitter.com/.
U.S. Department of Commerce. (2015). U.S. Census Bureau. Retrieved from http://www.census.gov/.
U.S. Environmental Protection Agency. (2015). Retrieved from http://www.epa.gov/.
Walsh, M. (2008). Worlds have collided and modes have merged: Classroom evidence of changed literacy practices. *Literacy*, 42(2), 101–108.
Wikipedia.org. (2015). Retrieved from https://www.wikipedia.org/.

Chapter 7

Research, Data Collection, and Analysis

The Internet can be used to help students research and gather information, however, teachers need to help their students be information literate. Although this is one way for students to conduct research, there are many other types of research that can be supported by digital tools that go beyond using the Internet as an electronic encyclopedia. Digital tools can be used to help students gather and analyze data, which can then be used to draw inferential conclusions to original research questions.

The purpose of this chapter is to provide an overview or foundation for using digital tools to support student research and will discuss ways that teachers can integrate digital tools to support students beginning to conduct original research, which includes information literacy, being able to define basic research question, gathering and analyzing data, and drawing inferential conclusions on their findings.

RESEARCH, DATA COLLECTION, AND ANALYSIS

Using a Web browser to gather information on the Internet can be a powerful research tool. The Common Core English/Language Arts Standards indicate that research and media are vital skills and themes for every grade level. "To be ready for college, workforce training, and life in a technological society, students need the ability to gather, comprehend, evaluate, synthesize, and report on information and ideas, to conduct original research in order to answer questions or solve problems, and to analyze and create a high volume and extensive range of print and non-print texts in media forms old and new" (Common Core State Standards Initiative, 2015, p. 4).

However, it is vital that students discriminate between good and bad information because it is easy to publish anything on the Internet and make it available globally. Students need to be able to locate credible informational sources and be able to do something with that information (i.e., organize and share it in a report, use it to make informed decisions, or help them build new understandings that then generate new questions to be investigated). Students must learn how to plan strategies that guide inquiry, so they can locate, organize, analyze, evaluate, synthesize, and ethically use information.

GATHERING AND EVALUATING SOURCES

Students can easily do a Google (2015a) search and find a great deal of information about their topic. Unfortunately, however, not all of the information is accurate or credible. In addition, because it is so easy for students to simply copy and paste the information they locate, they can plagiarize by using it as their own writing. Therefore, it is important to ensure that students understand what it means to be a good consumer of information and digital citizen in terms of responsible use of digital resources.

Although the Internet is the primary resource that students use today, it is important to help them understand that there are other informational resources (i.e., traditional print media). Although rapidly changing to digital delivery, newspapers, magazines, and books can still be a good sources for information that can broaden the student's research. Depending on the level of the students, teacher may also want to consider the use of peer-reviewed journal articles. These can be especially rich in terms of providing reviews of research projects.

Soon after the World Wide Web became widely available, it became clear that students needed to be able to evaluate research sources, especially Internet sources. Students must be clear about where they find information and who was responsible for creating it. Harris (2013) described Internet resources as being "on a continuum of reliability and quality" (p. 1), and provided the "CARS" checklist, which is a great resource for Web site evaluation in terms of *c*redibility, *a*ccuracy, *r*easonableness, and *s*upport.

In addition to the CARS model, there are online tutorials to help students understand how to evaluate Internet findings. One such tutorial is Houghton Mifflin's *Using the Web: Finding and evaluating Web sites* (2015). Although these tools will help students become good consumers of information found on the Internet, finding and appropriately citing credible information from the Internet is just the beginning of the research.

ORIGINAL RESEARCH

In addition to the vast amounts of information available from various Internet sources, students also need to be able to use digital tools to conduct original research by collecting data to help them answer questions and solve problems. Teaching students to conduct original research supports the notion of Lewis and Smith's (1993) definition of higher order thinking, "when a person takes new information and information stored in memory and interrelates and/or rearranges and extends this information to achieve a purpose or find possible answers in perplexing situations" (p. 136).

Conducting original research provides students with skills that will help them use digital tools to solve the complex issues and problems. However, teaching these skills requires teachers to be a bit more creative in developing lessons and units that engage their students in the research process. Conducting original research can be challenging and quite complex, and it is important to adjust the research complexity for the age and abilities of the students. However, with appropriate research questions, support, and scaffolds, original research can be conducted by students of any age.

RESEARCH AND DATA TYPES

Original research always begins with posing a research question. The type of research question determines the type of data one must collect to help answer that question. Research is about answering questions with data, sometimes it is information directly reported from others, such as information gathered from the Internet.

Other times research questions must be answered by collecting original or raw data from the "field." Collecting this kind of data from the original source supports real-life research by giving students responses to surveys, audio or video media files that when collected, reviewed, and analyzed will help answer the students research questions. However, it's important to understand that the research question will drive the research approach and subsequent data collection.

Quantitative Data

Data can be quantitative in nature, which might be the numerical results from a basic survey. Let's say for example that a teacher wants her high school students to achieve Common Core Math Statistics and Probability, specifically S-IC Making Inferences and Justifying Conclusions (Common Core State Standards Initiative, 2015b). A real-life research project might be to have students figure out if bullying is a problem at their school. The research question might be, "What percentage of the students believe that they have been a victim of bullying?"

To answer this question students will send out an anonymous survey to their peers, by having them create a survey using Google Forms (2015c). As the surveys are submitted, Google Forms creates a spreadsheet that calculates all of the data submitted, providing a percentage of students who believe they've been bullied. Although this is basic, notice that the question is really asking *how many*, which is a quantifiable element (i.e., a number). Once the data are collected, they can be analyzed in terms of mean median, and mode, thus helping students achieve CC Math S-IC by making inferences and using their data to justify their conclusions.

Qualitative Data

Data can also be qualitative in nature, meaning that it might be someone's response to an open-ended question, audio, or video from an observation or interview. Qualitative data is not generally quantifiable in nature. Rather, this data helps students *interpret* answers to their research questions. Qualitative data is often collected by social scientists and educators to help them describe or provide accounts of events or phenomenon in such a way as to help them draw inferences or interpretations of events. This can be more complex than a quantitative research project.

Let's say that a teacher wants his tenth graders to achieve outcomes listed in Common Core Language Arts writing standards for Literacy in History/Social Studies within the context of investigating Loyalists versus Revolutionaries during the American War for Independence. The specific outcome for Research to Build and Present Knowledge states: "Conduct short as well as more sustained research projects to answer a question (including a self-generated question) or solve a problem; narrow or broaden the inquiry when appropriate; synthesize multiple sources on the subject, demonstrating understanding of the subject under investigation" (Common Core State Standards Initiative, 2015a, p. 66).

The complexity of individual feelings and beliefs surrounding historical events from times past makes it difficult to gauge a student's understanding of what it might have been like to live during that time. People's perspectives have changed since the Revolution and with our twenty-first-century views, it is difficult to gain an understanding of how anyone could think it natural to be a *subject* of England's King George, or any king. Therefore, the research question might be: "How could it be natural to be considered a subject of a King?"

To answer this question, students would have to collect different types of data. In this case, qualitative data that might include historical records. Students might review art from the time, and primary and secondary source documents. However, reviewing and analyzing this data would most likely generate more questions, which could lead down other "avenues of exploration" thus supporting the outcome for "Research to Build and Present Knowledge."

They would then report their findings, which could take many forms, including a digitally published artifact. However, as the researchers, it is their *description* as supported by the qualitative data that brings meaning and context to the event or phenomenon being investigated. It is their written or published report that should convince the reader that their conclusions are accurate and valid and help answer the research question of what it was like to be a subject of King George.

DIGITAL DATA COLLECTION TOOLS

It is important to understand that research questions often require mixed methods, meaning that both quantitative and qualitative data may need to be collected to provide the broadest description or overview of the research topic. There are a variety of digital tools that students can use to collect both quantitative and qualitative data, which can then be organized and analyzed to help answer the research questions.

Scientific-Sensing Probes

Several companies support science education by providing scientific data collection devices, software, and educator resources. Vernier Software & Technology (2015) offers many different wired and wireless-sensing probes students can use to gather data (i.e., sensing light, temperature, motion, ultraviolet, gases, heart rate, motion, and a variety of others) and sent directly to iPads, smartphones, or laptops. They also provide software, curriculum, and even free software for science education from elementary through higher education.

Pasco (2015) is another company that offers scientific data collection devices, software, and educator resources. In addition to a variety of curriculum for physics, biology, chemistry, earth, environmental, and general science for high school, they also provide curriculum for middle and primary school science. DataStudio® is data collection and analysis software available for both Windows and Macintosh operating systems and provides real-time data collection and analysis from data collected from their various types of sensing probes.

Although these examples might provide great potential for learning, not every classroom will have access to these powerful data collection tools. Having limited resources shouldn't limit research learning activities. There are other ways to collect and record data (i.e., students can use traditional thermometers to collect temperature, which can then be recorded into a spreadsheet). Perhaps more importantly, data collection shouldn't be limited to simply numerical types of data.

Collecting data with more readily available tools can be used to support research and problem-solving learning activities as well. Students can collect still images, video, and even audio using digital cameras, or cell phones. Students can measure plant growth in height but also take a picture of it to illustrate the growth graphically. Or they might narrate verbally on their cell phones the growth that details their observations. Students should be taught to collect and analyze various types of data, using various data collection tools.

Survey Data Collection

Although there are commercial survey tools available, perhaps one of the best tools freely available for collecting survey data is Google Forms. Students can use the "Forms" tool, which is part of the suite of Google Docs to create a survey-style data collection form. Once the form is created it can be sent via e-mail, embedded into a Web page on Google Sites, or simply sent as a URL for others to complete. Form items include questions of various types, such as multiple choice, true/false, open-ended, ratings, and others. As participants complete the survey, data is automatically saved in a Google Docs spreadsheet.

Having students create, disseminate, and collect information in this manner can support research design, data collection, and analysis. Students could e-mail a form to their ePals in a different part of the country or world asking them to provide data on rainfall, temperature, or other quantifiable measures.

Multimedia Data Collection

Digital cameras, iPads, and Android tablets are great devices for gathering sounds, images, and videos, which can support qualitative data collection. In addition, smartphones have become commonplace in today's classrooms. Although some districts, schools, or teachers have issues with allowing students to use their smartphones in the classroom, these can be great multimedia data collection devices. Data collected in the form of digital files can be shared or sent from the smartphone to a variety of locations.

ORGANIZING AND ANALYZING TOOLS

Once data are collected, they need to be organized and analyzed to draw conclusions on what they might suggest or imply. There are several tools that students can use to do just that, some expensive and others that are freely available. Regardless of the organization or analysis tool, students should practice good file management, storage, organization, security, and safety.

File Storage

Although some schools have plenty of storage, there are also free *cloud* storage services for those students who have limited digital storage resources. While there are others, here are three examples. Microsoft OneDrive (2015b), Dropbox (2015), and Google Drive (2015b) provide storage that can be directly connected to one's computer or accessed only online. Once an account is created, students have access to free storage, where they can upload and organize their files into folders and subfolders. In addition, most storage services allow for sharing of folders or files with others, which supports collaborative projects.

Google Form Data Analysis

As mentioned before, Google Forms is an excellent tool for students to easily create and disseminate surveys. What might be even more powerful is that as the surveys are submitted, the data are automatically collected into a spreadsheet for analysis. Google Forms has a built-in data summary tool, but it can also be downloaded to a traditional spreadsheet. For example, the survey could ask students to reply to the following questions:

Please check the box for the number of times that you felt bullied this past week.
- Not at All
- One time
- Two times
- Three or Four times
- Every Day

Please check the box that corresponds to the possibility of you being bullied.
- No Chance
- It's Possible
- About Half
- A Very Good Chance
- Highly Possible

Once their data is available in a spreadsheet it can be viewed from various perspectives and displayed in a graphic manner for analysis that provides a graphic view for the learner. The actual data and graphic views of the results as shown in figure 7.1 provide the opportunity to "Use data from a sample survey to estimate a population mean or proportion; develop a margin of error through the use of simulation models for random sampling" (Common Core Standards Initiative, 2015a, p. 82).

Today's spreadsheets can house a variety of types of data within each cell, including formulas, which automatically apply mathematics functions to a group of cells, such as summing, averaging, and many others. In addition, to text and numerical data, most spreadsheets will also allow for multimedia files to be inserted as objects and thus allow students to include images, video, and audio.

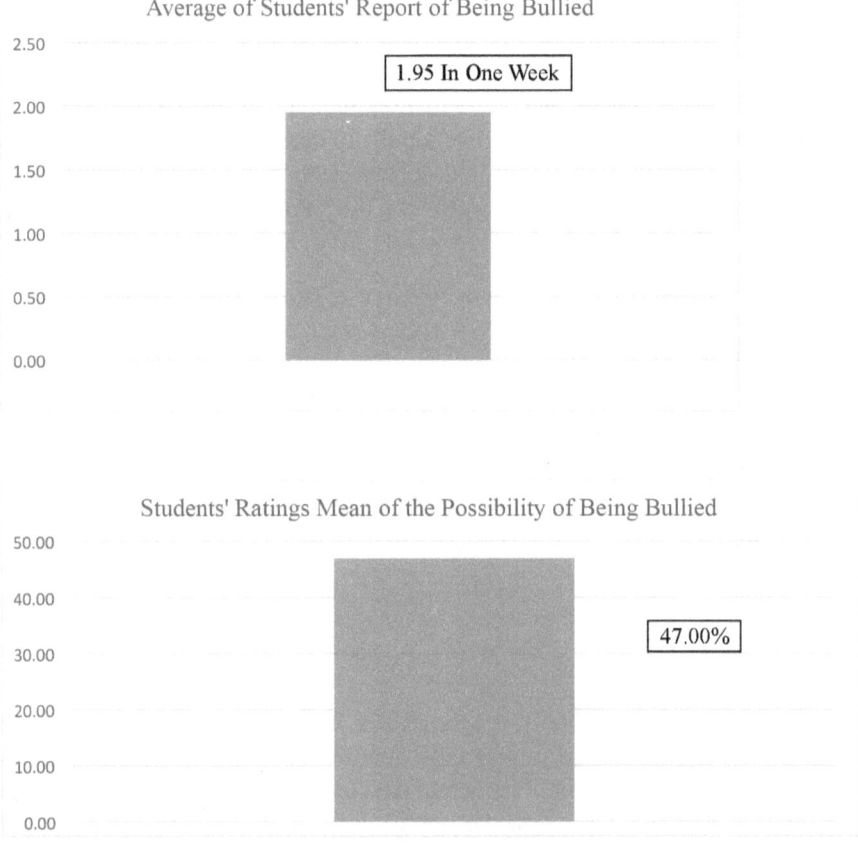

Figure 7.1 Spreadsheet Graphs

InspireData

One commercial tool that is designed specifically to help students in analyzing and organizing quantitative data is InspireData® (Inspiration Software Inc., 2015) and is available for Macintosh-and Windows-based computers. InspireData® provides students an easy to use data organization and analysis tool with many features. Students can enter their own data, select from various pre-entered data sets or import from other data sources, such as a spreadsheet. Data can then be manipulated and viewed in tables or plots, providing students with the opportunity to organize and view the data in various ways.

Databases

Although similar to a spreadsheet, databases can be used to collect and analyze more complex data. Your phone contacts list is an example of a database. A much more complex example, would be when you are doing online shopping. Most online stores use a complex database that allows you to search for specific items (i.e., color, size, etc.). Perhaps the most complex database example is Google.

Microsoft Access (2015a) and LibreOffice Base (The Document Team, 2015) are examples of powerful database programs, which are used by business and industry professionals, as well as educators. There are also some more simple freely available database programs. One example is Obvibase (2015), which can be added to your Google Suite of applications. In addition, Obvibase can save database files directly to your Google Drive or Dropbox storage areas. Obvibase might be a good option for students who want to get a beginning understanding of databases.

Helping students use a database program to collect and organize data can be challenging. However, there may be times when this type of application best serves your students. It really depends on what the lesson objectives are and how the tool can best help your students.

SCENARIO: RESEARCH AND DATA COLLECTION: ORAL HISTORIES

Michael is a tenth-grade history teacher in a modest high school with a fairly diverse student population. He and his students have pretty good access to technology, including eight classroom computers with Internet access. His school has a pretty good computer lab and technology support that provides additional tools, such as headsets, digital recorders, cameras, and even a few digital video cameras that can be checked out by teachers for student use.

Michael had heard about other teachers having their students gather "oral histories," where students interviewed people to hear them tell their life stories. He believed that this might be a good way to engage his students and help them meet the expectations of National Council for Social Studies Dimension 2: Change, Continuity and Context, specifically, "D2.His.1.9-12. Evaluate how historical events and developments were shaped by unique circumstances of time and place as well as broader historical contexts" (National Council for the Social Studies [NCSS], 2013, p. 46).

Michael found some great resources on oral history curriculum. The Tell Me Your Stories: An Oral History Curriculum (Living Legacies Historical Foundation, 2012) Web site and the Telling Lives Curriculum Guide (Albarelli and Starecheski, 2013) both provided unit plan ideas and methods that were helpful. Michael decided that it sounded interesting for his upcoming history unit on the Vietnam War Era and then found another great resource, specific to his topic. The Oral History Project of the Virtual Vietnam Archive (Texas Tech University, 2015) provided some resources, including some interview questionnaires.

Teachers at Michael's school work in teams of four, language arts, social studies, science, and mathematics, who all try to design integrated units between their disciplines as much as possible. Generally, one teacher will take the lead on a unit they feel most comfortable. The others then provide curriculum support as well as they can within their discipline. Michael then provided a few more details to his colleagues giving them the basics about his unit idea.

Michael explained that, although the students would be interviewing folks who lived in that era, they would first gather some information on specific events, prominent individuals, vocabulary specific to that time, and any other pertinent information that would help students create appropriate interview questions. Students would gather demographic information about the interviewees. Students would gather news media of events of the time, which could then be used along with the digital recordings of their interviews in their final video reports in the form of digital stories. After hearing the details, they agreed and offered their help.

Bill, the language arts teacher, was most excited and felt it would be a great cross-curricular collaboration for language arts and social studies and offered to develop language arts lessons that could be directly related to the unit. In particular, he thought that the unit would be great to help his students meet the Common Core: State Standards Initiative (2015a) for Writing #3 where students in grades 9 and10 are able to "Write narratives to develop real or imagined experiences or events using effective technique, well-chosen details, and well-structured event sequences" (Common Core: State Standards Initiative , 2015a, p. 46).

Jill, the mathematics teacher, also thought that it was a great idea and offered to add some statistics analysis lessons that would support any quantitative data analysis for the unit and suggested that she could design a lesson for her mathematics class where the students would interpret the quantitative data and analyze it to make inferences to justify conclusions about the findings, which were outlined in one of her standards. According to the Common Core: State Standards Initiative (2015b) for mathematics, High School Statistics and Probability: Interpreting Categorical and Quantitative Data, Making Inferences and Justifying Conclusions.

Finally, Sara the science teacher shared that her father was in Vietnam and had told her stories of the chemical *Agent Orange*, which was a defoliant used by soldiers to reduce the dense jungle foliage. She found the Make Agent Orange history: A humanitarian concern we can do something about website (Aspen Institute, 2012) and decided that her lessons would help the students achieve the Next Generation Science Standard "LS2.C: Ecosystems, Dynamics Functioning, and Resilience: What happens to an ecosystem when the environment changes?" (Achieve, 2015, p. 155).

Michael decided to break the unit process down into sections. First, students would conduct foundational research, which provided them with background information specific to the time, such as contextual terms, crucial events, and influential individuals and groups or organizations. Specifically, they would research contextual terms (i.e., Agent Orange, body count, fragging, and Hanoi Hilton, etc.), historical events (i.e., Tet Offensive, campus protests and shootings, My Lai, and Watergate, etc.), and individuals or groups (i.e., Ho Chi Minh, Richard Nixon, Viet Cong, and Students for a Democratic Society, etc.).

Next students would create a time-line and map to help see where and when these events happened. They were to identify certain locations (i.e., Saigon, Hanoi, 17th Parallel, DaNang, Khe Sanh, Laos, Thailand, and Cambodia, etc.). The students would use the foundational research findings to create interview questions. Students would also use the Virtual Vietnam Archive (Texas Tech University, 2015) to help guide their interview questions.

Michael asked the students to think about who in their family might best be a candidate to interview and reminded them that it could be a man or woman and that they didn't have to have served in the armed forces during the Vietnam War Era. They only had to have been living during that time and that they could recall some of their thoughts and feelings during the Vietnam War Era (1962–1972). Students who felt unable or uncomfortable conducting and recording interviews could listen to some of the Oral Histories on the Virtual Vietnam Archive (Texas Tech University, 2015).

Michael decided to have the students practice interviewing and recording one another so they would be familiar with the digital recording devices they planned on using. Most planned on using their smartphones to video record the interview. With the exception of one student, those who weren't using a smartphone had checked out the digital video cameras that they had used for the practice interview. One student's relative said that he would rather not be video recorded but was willing to have an audio recording made. This student then checked out a digital audio recorder from the school technical support lab.

Once the interviews were collected Michael would have each student watch his or her video interview alone, not taking any notes. Next, they would watch it again and this time making notes of first impressions of important things. Students then would watch their teammates' (teams of three) interviews making notes of first impressions and then discuss their notes and making lists of (or code) specific things that they agree on for each video, such as statements, concepts or beliefs such as: something that was repeated, something that seemed important to the interviewee, and something that was surprising.

Michael wanted to be able to assess each student's performance and achievement of his identified outcomes and decided to have them create an individual final report video. The final report video would include a video recorded narrative of the student, which included supporting multimedia evidence. The multimedia evidence included video clips from the recorded interviews, and historic images, audio or video clips found online.

To assess the students' achievement of the social studies and language arts standards, Michael and Bill worked together to first create a final video report criteria list to help structure their digital videos. This was given to the students before beginning writing their narrations and then assembling the video, which included the following.

In the written narrative the student demonstrates he or she can:

a. Introduce a topic clearly, previewing what is to follow; organize ideas, concepts, and information into broader categories as appropriate to achieving purpose; include formatting (i.e., headings), graphics (i.e., charts, tables), and multimedia when useful to aiding comprehension.
b. Develop the topic with relevant, well-chosen facts, definitions, concrete details, quotations, or other information and examples.
c. Use appropriate and varied transitions to create cohesion and clarify the relationships among ideas and concepts.
d. Use precise language and domain-specific vocabulary to inform about or explain the topic.
e. Establish and maintain a formal style and objective tone.
f. Provide a concluding statement or section that follows from and supports the information or explanation presented (Common Core State Standards Initiative, 2015a, p. 65).

The final video report criteria includes:

a. Audio narration and multimedia evidence (i.e., images, audio, or video).
b. Brief history of the Vietnam War that included descriptions of people, events, and locations.
c. Several key events and their impact.
d. An example of an effect of the Vietnam War and its specific cause.
e. An example of something that changed in society because of the Vietnam War.
f. Answers these questions: What events and turning points were important during the Vietnam War Era and why? How do people differ in their judgments about what was important during the Vietnam War Era? And Why do people differ in their judgments?

SUMMARY

The purpose of this chapter is to describe how digital tools can be used to help support engaging students in research, data collection, and analysis and in inquiry that requires students to do more than look up and report about information on the Internet. Using digital tools for research, data collection, and analysis can be used for many disciplines, but it is well suited for instruction using science inquiry.

The scenario for this chapter is a good example of how high school teachers worked together to create a thematic research unit that integrated social studies, language arts, math, and science. These teachers integrated digital tools and resources in a variety of ways, including quantitative and qualitative data collection, housing, analysis, and findings reporting. Although each teacher chose to use different tools resources and instructional strategies, they worked well together. Using these digital tools in this manner mirrors researchers in the field and gave these students historical inquiry experiences of real-life questions.

REFERENCES

Achieve, Inc. (2015). Next Generation Science Standards (NGSS): For states, by states. Retrieved from: http://www.nextgenscience.org/ms-ls2-4-ecosystems-interactions-energy-and-dynamics

Albarelli, G., and Starecheski, A. (2013). *Telling Lives Curriculum Guide.* Columbia University Center for Oral History. Retrieved from http://incite.columbia.edu/storage/Telling_Lives_Curriculum_Guide.pdf.

Aspen Institute. (2012). *Make Agent Orange history: A humanitarian concern we can do something about.* Retrieved from http://makeagentorangehistory.org/.

Common Core State Standards Initiative. (2015a). English and Language Arts Standards. Retrieved from http://www.corestandards.org/ELA-Literacy/.

Common Core State Standards Initiative. (2015b). Mathematics Standards. Retrieved from http://www.corestandards.org/Math/.

The Document Team. (2015). *LibreOffice* (Version 5.0.4) [Software]. Available from http://www.documentfoundation.org/.

Dropbox. (2015). Dropbox: Good things happen when your stuff lives here. Retrieved from https://www.dropbox.com/

Google. (2015a). Google. Retrieved from: http://www.google.com.

Google. (2015b). Google Drive: A safe place for all of your files. Retrieved from: https://www.google.com/intl/en/drive/.

Google. (2015c). Google Forms. Retrieved from: https://www.google.com/forms/about/.

Harris, R. (2013, December 27). Evaluating Internet research sources. Retrieved from: http://www.virtualsalt.com/evalu8it.htm.

Houghton Mifflin Company. (2015). Using the Web: Finding and evaluating Web sites. Retrieved from http://www.eduplace.com/kids/usingweb/g6-8.html.

Inspiration Software, Inc. (2015). InspireData: The visual way to explore and understand data. Retrieved from http://www.inspiration.com/InspireData.

Lewis, A., and Smith, D. (1993). Defining higher order thinking. *Theory into practice*, *32*(3), 131–137.

Living Legacies Historical Foundation (2012). An oral history curriculum. Retrieved from http://www.tellmeyourstories.com.

Microsoft. (2015a). Access. Database software and applications. Retrieved from https://products.office.com/en-us/access.

Microsoft. (2015b). OneDrive: One place for everything in your life. Retrieved from https://onedrive.live.com/about/en-us/.

National Council for the Social Studies (NCSS). (2013). The College, Career, and Civic Life (C3) Framework for Social Studies State Standards: Guidance for Enhancing Rigor of K–12 Civics, Economics, Geography and History. Silver Spring, MD: Author.

Obvibase. (2015). Obvibase: A truly simple database. Retrieved from https://www.obvibase.com/.

Pasco. (2015). DataStudio: 3-Axis accelerometer/altimeter. Retrieved from http://www.pasco.com/prodCatalog/PS/PS-2136_pasport-3-axis-accelerometer-altimeter/index.cfm.

Texas Tech University. (2015). The Vietnam Center and Archive: The oral history project. Retrieved from http://www.vietnam.ttu.edu/oralhistory/

Vernier Software and Technology, LLC. (2015). Retrieved from http://www.vernier.com.

Chapter 8

Creating and Publishing

When students use digital tools such as *Mindtools* (Jonassen, 2000), they engage in creative thinking and construct knowledge as they create and publish meaningful artifacts (Resnick, 1996). This chapter will provide examples of how students might use some of these digital tools (i.e., visualization tools to help them organize their thoughts by creating a cognitive map that outlines their understandings of a topic). Students can then use publishing tools to make meaningful products as they cement their understandings of that topic.

CREATING AND PUBLISHING

It is easy to think about using Internet tools to gather information and then a word processor or presentation software where students can produce a document that shows what they can do and what they have learned. However, there are many other technology tools that students can use that go far beyond finding information and putting it into a document. Let's think about how you might integrate technology tools in a student-centered manner in a more complex manner.

To learn new information, students need to think about their background knowledge on a topic; they can then begin to build on that knowledge or those understandings. Teachers often use a KWL chart to begin a new lesson to help their student learners begin to organize and plan their learning. They list what they know about the topic (K), what they want to learn about the topic (W), and then go back and review what they did learn about the topic (L). Table 8.1 is an example of a KWL chart, which helps students access and organize their background knowledge and plan out their learning goals for the upcoming lesson.

Although the KWL chart displayed in Table 8.1 provides students the opportunity to organize and plan their learning, there are technology tools that can do similar things, but perhaps more powerful for learning. Students can use visualization tools to help them organize their thoughts by making a cognitive map of what they know about a topic. Once they've listed the things they know about a topic, they can then begin to identify the things they don't know by listing or adding their ideas on the map, thus helping them outline what they need to learn.

As they research their topic using a variety of learning resources they can verify what they know and gather information about the things that they didn't know. In doing so, they must figure out how any new information fits into their former understanding. Then with the help of a publishing tool, students can build on their knowledge as they construct and assemble meaningful products. By creating meaningful products, they are given the opportunity to put the pieces together to demonstrate their new knowledge and understandings.

VISUALIZATION TOOLS

Students often have difficulties getting their ideas out on paper. Semantic or cognitive mapping has long been a strategy to help students organize their thoughts about a variety of topics, especially in the learning of language arts in elementary and middle school (Heimlich, 1986). Although students can create these with pencil and paper, there are several visualization tools that can help support a learner in developing a semantic or cognitive map. These include Kidspiration®, Inspiration® (Inspiration Software Inc., 2015), and cMap Tools (Institute for Human and Machine Cognition, 2015).

By using a visualization tool, students are supported in creating more dynamic models to help them explore more complex concepts, systems, or issues. As they create their cognitive map, students can organize ideas or

Table 8.1: KWL Chart

K	W	L
What I Already Know	What I Want Know	What I Learned
(Accessing Background Knowledge)	(Planning to Learn)	(Self-Assessment of Learning)

concepts graphically and think about possible connections between the elements.

Figure 8.1 illustrates how students might use Inspiration to organize what they know about a topic in terms of how the elements are connected to the central topic in various ways. The central topic is the U.S. Constitution and branches of government. Students can add things they know and then list items that will help them learn about the branches. Finding the answers will help guide their research. They can graphically visualize the various elements that they think might be part of the central topic organization and envision additional aspects, which helps them generate new ideas about that topic.

Images can be brought in from the clip art or copied and pasted from the Internet to help the learner reflect on and organize their thoughts about the topic. This view may help students who better visualize the topic in a graphic organizer, which has been recommended as a strategy to increase comprehension by using a common language (graphics) to better support English Language Learners (Reed and Railsbeck, 2003).

Perhaps the most powerful aspect of this type of digital visualization tool is that the cognitive map can be easily turned from a *graphic organizer* into

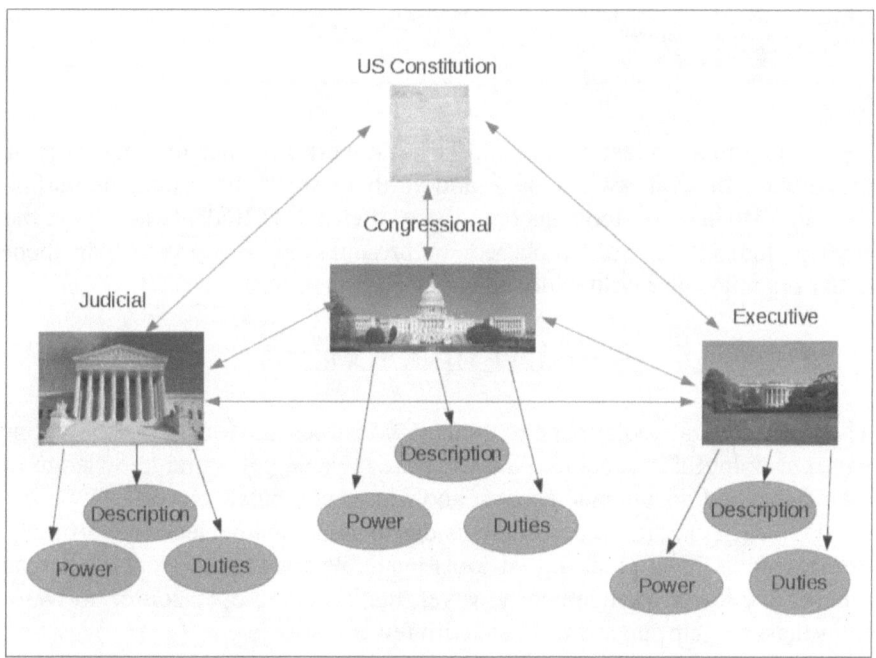

Figure 8.1 Graphic Organizer or Cognitive Map

an *outline* with the click of the mouse. By doing so, students can then see their graphic organizer in an outline format to see the hierarchical structure as shown. Being able to move back and forth between outline and graphic format allows students to view their cognitive map from various perspectives.

US Constitution and Branches of Government

1. Executive Branch

    a. Description
    b. Duties
    c. Power

2. Judicial Branch

    a. Description
    b. Duties
    c. Power

3. Congressional Branch

    a. Description
    b. Duties
    c. Power

Depending on a student's strength, they can work in either format—graphic or outline—or even switch back and forth to work in graphic or outline format. Visualization tools such as these often allow students to export the final outline into a word processor or presentation software to help them better organize their written document or presentation.

PUBLISHING TOOLS

There are several tools to help students construct knowledge as they construct meaningful product and demonstrate their thoughts and knowledge in their published documents. Most schools have computer labs or a few computers in each classroom that students use to create many electronic artifacts. Some schools have great digital tools available for their students, whereas others have fewer. Remember, however, that there are open source software titles that can help support teachers with fewer resources.

Document Creation

Word processors are often used by students to create documents that can demonstrate their understandings of specific content, as in a science report. Document creation has been shown to enhance the writing processes of students with learning disabilities (MacArthur, 1996). There are templates that can be downloaded to enhance word processors into powerful print publishing tools that support students in creating more robust and complex documents. In addition, there are print publishing tools, such as Microsoft Publisher (Microsoft, 2016), that support just about any kind of published product.

Students can use these templates to support their creation of many types of documents, including brochures, flyers, business cards, post cards, and newsletters, to name a few. For example, you might use the brochure template where your students create a volunteer environmental vacation brochure that details information on one of the earth's many global environmental issues. Today's word processors also allow for complex document formatting that support more innovative publications such as embedding multimedia, which can enhance meaningful products, making a word processor a powerful publishing tool.

Multimedia Editing and Creation

Student-developed multimedia biographies, where images, audio narratives, and video were collected or created, enhance student engagement and ownership in the learning activity (Jonassen, 2006). By creating an original multimedia artifact students are given the opportunity for personal or group expression in a more innovative and creative way to demonstrate their knowledge and or skills with the creation of presentations that include images, audio, and video. Presentation software is usually part of the productivity suites that schools might own or in open source software that can be downloaded for free.

Image Creation and Manipulation

Operating systems include an image-creation tool that can be used by students for creating or editing images (i.e., Paint in Windows). Students can use these basic image-creation tools to save images in a variety of file formats that can then be embedded or imported into other documents or multimedia presentations. Gimp (The Gimp Team, 2015) an open-source image-manipulation software is a powerful image-creation tool available for both the Macintosh and Windows computers that can be downloaded for free. Images captured using digital cameras or downloaded from the Internet can be manipulated to best suit the student's project.

Audio Creation and Manipulation

Operating systems also include basic sound recording software. However, one of the best free audio creation and manipulation tools is Audacity (2015). It can be downloaded and installed on most operating systems, and by using a built-in microphone or adding an inexpensive headset with microphone, it can be used to record, import, and edit audio files. Using audio in this fashion may be especially powerful for students with limited writing ability as a way to demonstrate their understandings by describing or narrating their thoughts.

Video Creation and Manipulation

Another powerful way to support student creativity is through video. Most laptop computers come with a camera and microphone that will record video and audio, which make video creation somewhat simple. In addition, students can use a movie-making program such as Apple's iMovie (2015b) and Window's Movie Maker (Microsoft, 2015). Although more robust video-creation and editing tools are commercially available, Movie Maker and iMovie are quite powerful when used in concert with audio- and image-editing software. Both can be used to create and edit video using various media files, including video clips, still images, and audio.

At the heart of Barrett's (2008) work on digital storytelling, she describes how students can use Movie Maker and iMovie to construct digital stories to create a video that requires them to organize information, write narration, and use multimedia. In addition to using advanced multimedia tools to edit audio, images, and video, digital storytelling provides students with the opportunity to create a portfolio element that demonstrates their understanding and reflect on their learning experience as they construct their meaningful product.

E-Books

Student-created e-books is another great way to demonstrate their understandings, especially literacy in both writing and technology. An e-book provides an excellent digital artifact that requires learners to demonstrate their skills at writing, layout, design, and be a bit more creative, as well.

Apple provides a free authoring tool called iBooks Author (Apple, 2015a), which when completed can be read on an iPad or computer with the latest Macintosh OS. It is quite powerful, yet easy to learn and provides the opportunity for students to demonstrate their writing but also supports embedding a variety of media, including images, audio, and video. Students can also save an iBooks Author file in PDF format, which allows for greater flexibility in sharing their work to those who do not have access to an iPad or Macintosh computer.

There are many other e-book authoring applications for both the iPad and Android-based tablets; some are more powerful than others. In addition, some word processors also have e-pub plug-ins, allowing to save a document created in the e-pub format, which can be read by many tablets and smartphones. Although this is a more affordable option if you don't have the resources, it is wise to try these tools out before having your students work with them. There are quite a few applications and plug-ins available that can be difficult to work with and could be frustrating for students.

SHARING PUBLISHED WORKS

Students will also benefit from sharing their newly acquired knowledge through a presentation to the class, which is an example of technology integration at a Type II application level (Maddux, Johnson, and Willis, 2001). Certainly, social media has provided a variety of venues for students to present and share their work. Although care does have to be taken when publishing to the general public, access can be limited to a safe, but more broad range of audience, such as ePals (2015), which helps teachers connect students in other schools and other countries.

Social Media

Social media has quickly become a way to share your thoughts, activities, photos, videos, and a variety of other elements of our lives. For example, Facebook provides a venue for one to share just about every aspect of ones' life. In addition, Twitter provides instant access to ones' thoughts in 140 characters. Although these applications are popular, and there are ways to integrate these into the classroom, there are other tools that might better serve for classroom publishing.

Wikis and blogs are Internet-based applications that permit students to individually or collaboratively publish. These tools also permit embedding images, audio, and video, thus making them multimedia-creation tools.

YouTube, podcasts, and vodcasts are publishing tools that are audio- or video-based. Podcasts are audio recordings in MP3 file format and can be listened to on an Apple iPod or directly from the Internet. By adding video, students can create their own vidcast or vodcast (video podcasts). Vodcasts, like podcasts, are watched on a video capable iPod or directly from the Internet.

Student-created podcasts or vodcasts can then be attached to discussion board postings, sent through e-mail, embedded within a blog or wiki to provide additional opportunities for students to publish their multimedia meaningful products. Doing so helps students communicate their ideas and information to a variety of audiences using a variety of media and formats.

Web-Based

Using Google Sites (Google, 2015) students can easily create a Web site where they publish their work and share it with a wider audience. Access to the site can be limited to only those invited or made public to the world. In addition, Google Sites, like all Google Docs, supports collaboration where students can co-author a site regardless of where they are in the world. Google Sites also supports multimedia and files can be attached for sharing.

iPads, Tablets, and e-readers

If students intend to share their e-books, it's important to know that there are several e-book file formats, which can only be read by specific e-readers. For example, the Kindle, generally uses the mobi format, whereas others might use e-pub. Therefore, it is wise to become familiar with the various file formats, readers, and tools that are available. However, a free e-reader app for phones and tablets for the various e-book file formats can generally be downloaded for free.

Sharing an e-book can be done in a variety of ways. Calibre (2015a) is an open-source electronic library management tool that can be housed on a computer connected to the Internet that allows users to access the e-books housed there. In addition, users can use Calibre to convert e-books from one format to another, which is a great feature because many e-book readers need the books to be in specific file formats. Calibre's online electronic library also provides for access control, so the sharing of the e-books can be limited or opened to the general public. This is a good way to protect, but still share, students' e-books.

SCENARIO: LANGUAGE ARTS PUBLISHING—E-BOOK LIBRARY

Juan is a twelfth-grade language arts teacher who works closely with the other language arts teachers in his high school. He often offered to have his writing students to work with the younger language arts classes to provide peer coaching. He thought that it would be a good experience for his students and provide help to their younger classmates. Although his fellow teachers liked the idea, they never seemed to be able to organize anything formal because of their various school schedules.

Juan sponsored an after-school writing club and the students had been experimenting with e-books and building an online e-book library. They began by acquiring free e-books, but also tried some authoring tools to create original ones. To make their library available, they downloaded and installed Calibre on an older computer that Juan's IT department provided. Juan also found that the Calibre Forum (2015b) provided e-book examples, a lot of technical support, and ideas of how to best use Calibre.

Calibre is a free open-source e-book library software that houses, manages, and allows for online e-book delivery. Once uploaded to the Calibre Library, e-books can be downloaded from the Web to a computer or e-book reader. In addition, the online Calibre Library can be secured with user accounts and passwords, thus protecting the students' work. They soon discovered that different e-book readers require different file formats, but one of Calibre's functions is e-book format conversion for various readers. Although not perfect, it allowed the writing club members to get a better sense of how various e-book readers displayed the various formats.

Juan thought that this might be the opportunity to provide the peer coaching and brought up the idea with his writing club. He then asked them to think about how that might work. They were quick to come up with some ideas. If the other grade-level teachers would be willing to have their students create their writing using an e-book publishing tool, they could then submit them to the writing club's Calibre library for publication and sharing. The writing club students could then review and provide feedback on the writing.

Juan explained to his writing club that his fellow faculty might need some technical support to help their students use an e-book authoring tool and the Calibre online library. The writing club members had been using iBooks Author. Although free from Apple, it only runs on Apple products (i.e., Macintosh and iPads). He suggested that they think about an inexpensive app that students could easily learn to use that might run on Android. After a brief search, they found the Educade Web site (2016), which illustrates how students can create e-books using Creative Book Builder (2015), an inexpensive app for both iPads and Android tablets.

Juan had his writing club present the idea and demonstrate how Calibre worked to house and manage e-books. They also demonstrated how students might use several e-book authoring tools—iBooks Author and Creative Book Builder. Although writing would be the main focus of the e-books, these tools also support adding images, audio, and video, thus allowing students to create multimedia e-books. The writing club also offered to provide after-school tutorials on how to use these tools as well as peer coaching for writing. Juan's fellow faculty were impressed and decided to give it a try.

To help things get started, Juan suggested to his fellow faculty that they should think about the kinds of writing they would be requiring in their classes. He mentioned that the writing club would be willing to provide peer coaching on any topic and any genre (i.e., reports, prose, poetry, etc.). However, he suggested that the teachers simply plan their writing lessons based on the language arts standards they would normally have as lesson outcomes, and that these should be shared with his writing club students so they would have a better sense of the criteria each teacher will be expecting.

The teachers could have their students write using traditional word processors and then share their work with the writing club students for peer coaching. Once the work was finalized, unless the final product could not be submitted in an e-book format, the manuscript would be published using either iBooks Author or Creative Book Builder along with any multimedia that was appropriate for the assignment. These published e-books would then be uploaded to the Calibre server to be shared with the appropriate faculty, students, and perhaps parents.

SUMMARY

The focus of this chapter is to provide an overview of how students might construct knowledge with the help of visualization and publishing tools in the creation and sharing of meaningful artifacts or products. The chapter provided examples of digital tools that support the creation of documents, e-books, Web sites, and multimedia. The chapter also provided examples of how students might present or share their work through a variety of technology tools designed to help students publish their work.

Designing lessons that integrate technology to support student creativity and publishing might require some creativity. The scenario presented provided an example of how a teacher might have students use current e-book authoring tools to help support student publishing within a school. The scenario described how a student club might provide technical expertise and coaching for younger writers using current e-book authoring and publishing tools to create and share their published works.

Having an extracurricular group perform this service gave these students the opportunity to experiment with creative and publishing tools. With no real academic standards to meet for the extracurricular group, Juan had more freedom in how he organize the project. However, the students in the writing club would still be aware of appropriate grade-level writing standards for the students they would be coaching. Finally, by having the opportunity to publish their work, electronically, all students would be learning writing and sharing their work using creation and publishing tools.

REFERENCES

Apple. (2015a). iBooks Author. Retrieved from http://www.apple.com/.
Apple. (2015b). iMovie. Retrieved from http://www.apple.com/.
Audacity. (2015). Audacity: Free audio editor and recorder. Retrieved from http://audacity.sourceforge.net/.
Barrett, H. (2006). Digital storytelling tools. Retrieved from http://electronicportfolios.com/digistory/tools.html.
Calibre. (2015a). E-book management. Retrieved from http://calibre-ebook.com/.

Calibre. (2015b). Calibre forum. Retrieved from http://www.mobileread.com/forums/forumdisplay.php?f=166.
Educade. (2016. Teaching tool. Retrieved from http://www.educade.org/teaching_tools/creative-book-builder.
ePals. (2015). Where learners connect. Retrieved from http://www.epals.com/.
Google. (2015). Google Sites. Retrieved from https://www.google.com/.
Heimlich, J. E. (1986). *Semantic mapping: Classroom applications. Reading Aids Series.* IRA Service Bulletin, Book no. 230. Newark, DE: International Reading Association.
Inspiration Software Inc. (2015). Inspiration. Retrieved from http://www.inspiration.com.
Institute for Human and Machine Cognition. (2015). *cMap tools.* Retrieved from http://cmap.ihmc.us\.
Jonassen, D. (2006). *Modeling with technology: Mindtools for conceptual change* (3rd ed.) Upper Saddle River, NJ: Merrill Prentice Hall.
Jonassen, D. H. (2000). *Computers as Mindtools for schools: Engaging critical thinking* (2nd ed.). Upper Saddle River, NJ: Merrill Prentice Hall.
MacArthur, C. A. (1996). Using technology to enhance the writing processes of students with learning disabilities. *Journal of Learning Disabilities, 29*(4) 344–354.
Maddux, C. C., Johnson, D. L., and Willis, J. W. (2001). *Educational computing: Learning with tomorrow's technologies* (3rd ed.). Needham Heights, MA: Allyn and Bacon.
Microsoft. (2015). Movie Maker. Retrieved from http://windows.microsoft.com/en-US/windows-live/movie-maker.
Microsoft. (2016). Publisher. Retrieved from https://products.office.com/en-us/publisher.
Ng, T. (2015) Creative Book Builder v32 (CBB). Retrieved from http://getcreativebookbuilder.blogspot.com.
Reed, B., and Railsbeck, J. (2003). *Strategies and resources for mainstream teachers of English language learners.* Retrieved August 11, 2008, from http://www.nwrel.org/request/2003may/ell.pdf.
Resnick, M. (1996). *Distributed constructionism.* In Proceedings of the 1996 international conference on learning sciences (pp. 280–284). International Society of the Learning
The Gimp Team. (2014). Gimp—The GNU image manipulation program. Retrieved from http://www.gimp.org/.

Chapter 9

Thinking Critically: Solving Problems and Making Decisions

Through visual representations, today's digital tools and educational software can provide opportunities for students to examine, investigate, practice, or explore activities, which might be dangerous, expensive, too difficult, or just simply impossible for students. By using case-based, project-based, inquiry-based, and problem-based learning strategies, teachers can engage their students in ways that support learning at a deeper level, critical thinking, problem solving, and decision making.

This chapter will provide examples of using digital tools and how they can support students as they begin to tackle real-life issues and problems. Through the integration of simulations, scenarios, exploratory, and logical thinking tools, students can practice, explore, and manipulate complex concepts and try out their ideas in a safe environment, which helps them gain more accurate understandings.

CRITICAL THINKING, PROBLEM SOLVING, AND DECISION MAKING

Making knowledgeable decisions that help solve real-world problems requires that a person is able to explore and identify various solutions from a variety of perspectives. To help students learn these skills, teachers have used case-based, project-based, inquiry-based, or problem-based instructional strategies, where students are engaged in research of some kind, analyzing findings, and applying their knowledge and skills to visualize solutions and making decisions.

The general difference between these instructional strategies is how the teacher structures the learning environment in terms of responsibility for learning. Depending on grade level, cognitive abilities, and the specific instructional strategy employed, the teacher may provide more or less structure. A problem-based learning activity may only provide an "ill-structured" problem requiring students to organize and control all aspects of the learning activity. When employing a project-based unit, the teacher might provide roles with specific tasks, detailed step-by-step instructions for the process, and detailed instructions for students to follow.

Using an instructional strategy that provides less structure gives students more control for learning decisions and requires them to think more critically, organize more thoroughly, solve problems as they arise, and make decisions (i.e., carry out all aspects of the learning process). That is, teachers are then using an instructional strategy that provides greater structure, which supports students who may not be ready or able to do those things. Selecting the appropriate instructional strategy should be based on the students. However, it's important to help them take more control of the learning process in these strategies so they can begin to gain these higher-order thinking skills.

TOOLS FOR EXPLORATION

There are instructional strategies and educational software programs that provide opportunities to enhance critical thinking, problem solving, and decision making, which foster higher-order thinking skills. These tools can provide a safe virtual environment where students can learn in ways that allow them to investigate concepts, manipulate variables, and try out their thoughts. By integrating scenarios and simulations, teachers can support students' exploration using scenarios and simulations, where students explore ideas, concepts, and methods.

Scenarios

Creating a scenario can provide structured support for project-based learning. Often times, however, scenarios of this type are not digital scenarios, but rather students use digital tools to investigate and create final products for the scenario. A quick Internet search for two of the classic scenarios: Dream Vacation and Travel Agent will yield some great lesson and unit plans that integrate a variety of subjects.

In the Dream Vacation scenario, students are given the task of planning a vacation where they must design an itinerary and gather information that includes cost for transportation, housing, food, and entertainment. Students gather other information, such as local events, historical sites, geographical elements weather, or demographics (depending on how the teacher wants to integrate other subjects). Often, students are also required to create a spreadsheet budget.

In the Travel Agent scenario, students conduct similar searches, but then use a digital publishing tool to create an advertisement brochure, a Web site, or video commercial that includes all of the required information. Students engage in Internet searches to gather information and media, which is then put into some form of digitally published advertisement.

These are just two examples that have been used by many teachers. However, it's important to remember that the key to designing a good scenario is in how well the students are engaged in the *process* of thinking critically to investigate issues, making decisions, and solving problems, not just creating a cool final product. There are many online resources for integrating scenarios in your classroom, including Scenario Based Learning (WikiEducator, 2011); How to engage learners with scenario-based learning (Kovi and Spiro, 2013); and Three ways to use scenarios (Bean, 2010).

Simulations

Simulations are virtual settings that allow students to explore and try out ideas, concepts, and skills that might otherwise be too expensive or possibly dangerous. The classic simulation is the computerized flight simulator that allows students to try flying a plane without injury on crashing. Another classic is the online frog dissection. Indeed, there are quite a few virtual labs available that provide a variety of simulations for biology, chemistry, and others. Although many require a paid subscription, there are also free virtual labs, and a quick Internet search will provide some great resources.

In addition to the variety of virtual labs, there are other types of digital simulations, which provide digital exploration. Geometer's Sketchpad (McGraw-Hill Education, 2014) is a good example. Geometer's Sketchpad is an educational software program (available for PC, Mac, and online) that students can use to explore geometric theorems.

Often students find it difficult to understand how, in Euclidean Geometry, the sum of the angles of a triangle always equal 180 degrees. Because the tool allows the user to manipulate the graphic, students can grab and drag one of the corners of the triangle, thus changing the angles, however, the total still always equals 180 degrees. By being able to manipulate triangles in this way, students can engage in a much more concrete exploration of this concept of geometry, physically manipulating and then visually seeing the results, which provide images that help meaning within the learning of mathematics (Furner and Marinas, 2007).

Students using these types of digital tools are given the opportunity to explore ideas and concepts and develop and try out models. In doing so, they can virtually see examples of constructs that without those tools must be conceptually visualized. In this way students begin to construct their understanding of complex concepts and ideas with the help of more concrete manipulative visual representations that might otherwise require more formalized operational cognitive development (Piaget, 1976).

Using a simulation to exploring concepts or ideas, students are able to make decisions and control variables and see the results. Students are able to compare and contrast how changing a variable might influence or impact an element or situation, giving them the opportunity to make decisions and see the results. If the results are not favorable, they can remake the decisions to see how things might change, thus learning safely from their mistakes. There are several online resources that support using simulations in the classroom, including Teaching with simulations (Blecha, 2013) and Use simulations to help students learn (Creativeteachingsite.com, 2011).

TOOLS FOR LOGICAL THINKING

Designed by Wally Feurzeig and Seymour Papert, LOGO (Chakraborty, Graebner, and Stocky, 1999) was originally a drawing program that gave students the opportunity to write code that would direct movements of an object, called the "turtle," which would then be traced with pen and paper. LOGO was then improved, allowing students to design the path that the turtle would take around the computer screen by writing specific computer programming commands. The purpose was to use a computer program to help students learn by first figuring out the path they wanted the turtle to take and then transfer that into the computer programming language.

Although newer computer applications have become much more sophisticated, many still use similar programs and programming languages. Turtle Academy (2015) is a free interactive Web site that teaches programming principles for children across the globe. Math Playground's (2014) Math Programming interactive Web site provides a LOGO game that allows students to write code to move the turtle around the screen. There are examples that students can copy and paste into the command line to see how the program works. Students can then explore how LOGO works using their own commands.

The MIT Education Arcade (Scheller Teacher Education Program, 2015) provides a variety of educational resources, including free games, simulations, and digital tools designed to help students build math and science skills. StarLOGO TNG (MIT STEP, 2015), a visual programming environment for games and simulations, was developed on the principles of the original LOGO but uses a three-dimensional graphical interface. This interface allows students to see and explore the concepts of simulations and complex systems through drag-and-drop methods rather than abstract written commands of previous computer programming languages.

SCENARIO: CRITICAL THINKING, PROBLEM SOLVING, AND DECISION MAKING—PLANETARY PLANNING

Marcus is a tenth-grade social studies teacher in a suburban school. Although he's given some resources, he often has to come up with curriculum that is exciting and engaging for his students. Over his spring break Marcus had the opportunity to attend a conference that focused on technology integration. During one of the sessions he attended the presenters suggested that teachers should give their students more responsibility for decisions and direction in the use of the digital tools they used to construct projects. Marcus decided to design a problem-based learning with limited structure for three reasons.

First, Marcus believes that by giving his students less structure they will be required to take more control and thus more responsibility for their learning. In doing so, Marcus believes that his students will be engaged at a much deeper level because they have to plan, organize, define and assign tasks, monitor progress, and develop materials that will help them communicate their conclusions about their informed actions.

Second, Marcus believes that his high school students will be able to take control of their learning or can learn the organizational skills to manage themselves within the problem-based learning environment that this scenario describes. However, he also knows that he will need to partner with his students by carefully observing and providing guidance, scaffolds, and feedback to help support them as they engage in this constructivist learning environment.

Finally, he believes that it is important to give his students greater responsibility for their learning by letting them select and use technology tools that will best support their endeavors. Therefore, he only provided a list of "Suggested Tools for Success," which outlined the *types* of digital tools that might be used for specific organizational and procedural tasks. In doing so, Marcus believes he will be giving his students the opportunity to examine these technology tools and make decisions on how best to employ them to be successful in the learning task.

In this scenario, students are asked to produce products that address specific topics and elements that are drawn from the four C3 dimensions because they are requirements embedded within the *conditional planetary member application*. As such, this scenario provides assessment criteria but does not provide organizational and procedural structure. In other words, students in this scenario are given pretty specific criteria for what they are to produce, but only suggestions for tools to help them produce it, and little or no guidance for how they will organize themselves or the process (steps) they will need to go through to complete the task.

Because his district requires that students achieve the College, Career, and Civic Life C3 Framework (National Council for the Social Studies [NCSS], 2013) Marcus decided that he would design a scenario-based unit around the framework's four dimensions: Develop Questions and Plan Inquiries; Apply Disciplinary Tools and Concepts (i.e., civics, economics, geography, and history); Evaluate Sources and Use Evidence; and Communicate Conclusions and Take Informed Action.

Marcus began by creating the following documents to set the stage for his unit and provide the background for the scenario and the criteria for products the students would produce.

- The Extraterrestrial Communique
- Conditional Planetary Membership Guidelines
- Suggested Tools for Success

The Extraterrestrial Communique

In the early part of the twenty-first century a communique was received by the Search for Extraterrestrial Intelligence (SETI) receivers sent by alien emissaries representing the United Planets of the Milky Way (UPMW). The communique was an official invitation for the citizens of the planet Earth to submit a conditional planetary member application to join as a member of the UPMW.

After getting over much amazement, the various governments of Earth organized a global response team to conduct formal negotiations to gain a better understanding of who the aliens were and how best to respond to the communique. It was discovered that the UPMW was a benevolent governing body for the Milky Way Galaxy, whose scientists had been observing Earth and found its inhabitants (us) were now ready to become aware of other life in the galaxy, their governing community, and to possibly gain membership.

As the response team gathered more information it was discovered that if the conditional planetary member application was approved by the Milky Way Planetary Admissions Council (MWPAC), *conditional membership* would be granted. After ten years of successful membership, the *conditional* planetary member could apply for *continuing* planetary membership.

There were some social benefits to conditional membership, but the UPMW had strict rules about changing a newly admitted planet too quickly, in terms of providing advances in medical, technical, and even social elements. Therefore, the conditional planetary member application had specific rules and requirements. The following document outlines the conditional application guidelines and suggested tools for success.

Conditional Planetary Member Application Guidelines

To submit a conditional planetary member application to the UPMW, the inhabitants of the applicant planet must abide to the following three stipulations.

First, as the planet's youth are the future planners and decisions makers of the planet's society, it is important to gain an understanding if the inhabitants' beliefs and understandings of certain issues are in alignment to all cultures within the UPMW. Therefore, the conditional planetary member application must be developed by students working in teams within the educational systems.

This stipulation of the application process will help the MWPAC evaluate how well young people and possible future members of the UPMW understand diverse cultures, societal issues, and are able to work collaboratively to overcome differences and issues. Because membership in the UPMW often requires collaboration between many diverse cultures, these are vital skills.

Second, the conditional planetary member application must address specific aspects, topics, or issues. Specifically, the application must describe how science and technological advances have impacted your planet, in terms of its inhabitants from many perspectives. To be successful, the conditional planetary member application must clearly address and include *all* of the following elements:

a. Identify and provide both current and historical examples of the interaction and interdependence of science, technology, and society in a variety of cultural settings.
b. Judge and provide an opinion of how science and technology have transformed the physical world and human society and the understanding of time, space, place, and human-environment interactions.
c. Analyze and provide an opinion of how science and technology influence the core values, beliefs, and attitudes of society, and how core values, beliefs, and attitudes of society shape scientific and technological change.
d. Evaluate and detail various policies that have been proposed as ways of dealing with social changes resulting from new technologies, such as genetically engineered plants and animals.
e. Identify and interpret various perspectives about human societies and the physical world using scientific knowledge, ethical standards, and technologies from diverse world cultures.
f. Formulate strategies and suggest policies for influencing public discussions associated with technology–society issues, such as the greenhouse effect.

Third, the conditional planetary member application must be created using the most current information/communication technology the planet has to offer. This is to demonstrate young people's creativity and their ability to use the most current technology to research, organize, present, and share information. Furthermore, by using digital tools, the application will be more easily submitted to the MWPAC through electronic digital transmission.

Suggested Tools for Success

The conditional planetary member application is a complex task, but one that can be completed by working together using tools that the inhabitants of the planet are using. Although some individuals on the planet have demonstrated poor use of some of these powerful tools, others have shown that they can be helpful in working together to gather, organize, judge, and present the information required on the conditional planetary member application. To successfully complete this task we suggest that you use the following tools.

Planning Tools

Use these tools to help you visualize the information you already know, the information that needs to be investigated, ideas about how you will organize the investigation, the steps you will need to take to complete the application, who might take on the various required tasks, and other things that you might need to consider to be successful.

Communicating and Collaborating Tools

Use these tools to help you organize and form your investigation teams. Use these tools to build social networks to build consensus about how you will approach and write the conditional planetary member application. Use this tool as a clearinghouse that will foster communication and collaboration between teams to share ideas, work flow and content elements of your conditional planetary member application.

Research and Data Collection Tools

Use these tools to investigate and gather information on the impact that science and technology advances have had on the individuals, societies, and cultures of your planet and the impact individuals, society, and cultures have had on science and technology advances on your planet. Remember, you need to investigate all of the topic areas from both perspectives for the conditional planetary member application.

Data Organizing and Analysis Tools

These type of tools can be used to help you organize and analyze data, resources, or media that you collect. For example, you may want to use them to organize and list team members, task roles, and other data to help you keep track of the personnel working on the conditional planetary member application. You may also want to use these tools to help your team house or store the gathered resources and media examples to help organize, prioritize, as well as provide additional information about the examples collected, (i.e., The quote by John F. Kennedy from his inaugural address, 1/20/1961 would help identify "Ask Not . . ." JFK video clip.).

Multimedia Editing and Authoring Tools

These types of tools can help you create or edit media that will be used to present and support your investigation findings. These will be used to help create and develop multimedia files (i.e., images, audio, and video), which will be embedded into the application. The final version of your conditional planetary member application must be in a published form. Therefore, you will want to select and use an authoring tool that will best support a quality published application.

SUMMARY

The purpose of this chapter is to provide examples of various digital tools that students can use to support their critical thinking, problem solving, and decision making. Integrating these digital tools is described from mostly a student-centered perspective. Depending on the grade level, instructional strategy implemented, and cognitive abilities of the students, this requires the teacher to provide more or less structure.

In providing less structure, students will have more control and responsibility, and the teacher will be required to provide appropriate scaffolds as needed. Doing so requires teachers to relinquish control and responsibility for the learning to the students. The chapter also included examples of digital tools used for exploration and logical thinking, including scenarios and simulations, which provide context.

The scenario for this chapter took a problem-based learning approach that provided little structure for the students as they went through the unit. The teacher designed the unit so the students would have to take responsibility for the learning process. However, the teacher was also available to answer questions, provide suggestions, and pose thought-provoking questions to help support their critical thinking about the learning task and the technology tools they plan on using to best present their knowledge of how science, technology, and society interact and impact one another.

In taking this approach, his students would be supported through their collaboration as members of teams. The scenario did not outline or describe how the activity was structured to encourage individual accountability and group interdependence. Rather in this scenario the responsibility to organize and structure the teams, and tasks is left open-ended.

Another approach would be to provide more structure by requiring specific technology tools and teaming requirements. Team member roles could be defined, where each student within a team would be responsible for a specific aspect of the task (i.e., researcher, a data warehouse specialist, a multimedia specialist, a communication specialist, and a production manager). Specific digital tools could have been defined (i.e., Internet for information gathering, Dropbox for date storage for media files, e-mail for communication, and Google Sites as a publishing tool).

By adding more structure, the teacher takes more control from the students, who will then have less responsibility for the learning task. In addition, requiring specific digital tools for specific technology tasks limits the students' opportunities to explore how different tools can be used to complete various tasks. Providing more structure to support students in the project may well have implications for their learning experience, in terms of learning to think critically, solve problems, and make decisions.

REFERENCES

Bean, C. (2010). Kineo city and guilds group: Three ways to use scenarios. Retrieved from http://www.kineo.com/us/resources/top-tips/learning-strategy-and-design/three-ways-to-use-scenarios

Blecha, B. (2013). Teaching with simulations. Pedagogy in Action. Retrieved from http://serc.carleton.edu/sp/library/simulations/index.html.

Chakraborty, A., Graebner, R., and Stocky, T. (1999). Logo: A project history. Retrieved from http://web.mit.edu/6.933/www/LogoFinalPaper.pdf.

CreativeTeachingSite.Com. (2011). Educational simulations: Use simulations to help students learn. Retrieved from: http://www.creativeteachingsite.com/edusims.html.

Furner, J. M., and Marinas, C. A. (2007). Geometry sketching software for elementary children: Easy as 1, 2, 3. *Eurasia Journal of Mathematics, Science & Technology Education*, 3(1), 83–91.

Kovi, H., and Spiro, K. (2013). How to engage learners with scenario-based learning. *Learning Solutions Magazine*. Retrieved from http://www.learningsolutionsmag.com/articles/1108/how-to-engage-learners-with-scenario-based-learning.

MathPlayground.com. (2014). Math programming. Retrieved from http://www.mathplayground.com/mathprogramming.html.

McGraw-Hill Education. (2014). Geometer's sketchpad. Retrieved from http://www.dynamicgeometry.com/.

MIT STEP. (2015). StarLogo TNG. Massachusetts Institute of Technology: Scheller Teacher Education Program Retrieved from http://education.mit.edu/projects/starlogo-tng.

National Council for Social Studies (NCSS). (2013). The College, Career, and Civic Life (C3) Framework for Social Studies State Standards: Guidance for Enhancing Rigor of K–12 Civics, Economics, Geography and History. Silver Spring, MD: Author.

Piaget, J. (1976). Piaget's theory. In The grasp of consciousness: Action and concept in the young child (pp. 11–23). Berlin: Springer.

Scheller Teacher Education Program. (2015). MIT Education Arcade. Retrieved from http://education.mit.edu/.

TurtleAcademy. (2015). Learn LOGO programing in your browser. Retrieved from https://turtleacademy.com/.

WikiEducator. (2011). Scenario based learning. Retrieved from http://wikieducator.org/Scenario_Based_Learning.

Chapter 10

Digital Games for Learning

Educational software publishers realized and have been taking advantage of the motivational aspect of including gaming elements in their educational software for decades. An old example, Oregon Trail (Houghton Mifflin Harcourt, 2015), allows students to "win" by surviving the virtual journey, and the hunting-for-food element is similar to the first-person shooter video games of today. The chapter sheds light on the various types of games, the impact gaming has on learning, and provides some ideas of how to take advantage of the motivation and the benefits it may offer when integrated into classroom learning.

DIGITAL GAMES FOR LEARNING

There are a variety of video games and there are many ways to integrate them into a classroom, therefore it's important to understand how each might impact students. Teachers should be knowledgeable about how to take advantage of the motivation and benefits a game may offer, but at the same time know how the game can *safely* support their learning objectives. Will the game be for exploring a new concept, practicing skills, or to support higher-order learning such as critical thinking, problem solving, and decisions making? Are there issues with game play in the classroom?

ISSUES OF GAME PLAY

Mainstream media have published articles that outline the benefits of game play in learning and also articles listing the risks or detriments of video gaming. The research suggests that effects of game play are more complex and the impact of game play is often dependent on video types, a player's interests, and the behaviors being investigated (Bavelier, et al., 2011).

There is some evidence that excessive gaming is correlated to aggressive behavior and is potentially addictive, especially in adolescents (Grüsser, Thalemann, and Griffiths, 2006). Others are convinced that violent video game play creates a risk factor for violent behavior and public policy should focus on how to best deal with that. (Anderson, et al., 2010) However, Yousafzai, Hussain, and Griffiths (2013) stated that although it is clear that in some people a technology addiction, like gambling, may manifest in different ways.

Although there may be issues with game play in the classroom, there may also be merit to motivating students to engage in a learning activity. However, it is important that game play in the classroom have an academic purpose. There should be a purpose, rationale, and intentionality.

In addition, it is important to be judicious in game choice because some games can carry added issues. Schwartz (2014) details a social studies teacher, who states that using Skyrim (Bethesda Softworks LLC, 2015) produces rich discussions and enhances the thinking level of his students. However, Skyrim is a role-playing game that includes adult themes such as blood, gore, violence, sex, and alcohol. Although this might work well for this teacher, the students in his classroom, and within his particular school and district, it could easily be an issue for many parents.

GAME-BASED LEARNING

There are, however, many who believe that game-based learning can motivate and engage students in fun and challenging ways, but it should have some element of entertainment. (Dai and Wind, 2011) Other educational experts describe it from a more student-centered approach and suggest that teachers think about their students *playing* and *learning* rather than being entertained (Resnick, 2004). Others, although agreeing with the value of game-based learning, also suggest the need for structure, guidance, direction, or scaffolding during instruction. (Kirschner, Sweller, and Clark, 2006; Klahr and Nigam, 2004; Mayer, 2004)

Van Eck (2009) describes using commercial off-the-shelf games for learning, outlines the notion of game-based learning, and provides five philosophical premises:

1. The teacher is technologically competent and assumes the roles of designer, manager, and facilitator.
2. The student actively engages in the learning process, assumes the role of researcher, and becomes technologically competent.

3. The computer is used as a tool, as it is in the workplace, to enhance learning through the use of real-world data to solve problems.
4. The lesson is student-centered, problem-based, and authentic, and technology is an integral component.
5. The environment incorporates multiple resource-rich activities.

GAME-BASED LEARNING RESOURCES

- Game-Based Learning Units for the Everyday Teacher http://www.edutopia.org/blog/video-game-model-unit-andrew-miller
- How to Plan Instruction Using the Video Game Model http://www.edutopia.org/blog/how-to-plan-instruction-video-game-model-judy-willis-md
- How Online Simulations work in the Classroom http://www.edutopia.org/online-simulations-classroom
- Ten Ways Teachers are Using MMORPGs in the Classroom http://www.teachthought.com/trending/10-ways-teachers-are-using-mmorpgs-in-the-classroom/
- MinecraftEdu provides products and services that make it easy for educators to use Minecraft in the classroom. http://minecraftedu.com/about

GAME TYPES

Often people believe that games fall into two categories, education or entertainment, with some being somewhere in the middle (i.e., edutainment). However, the gaming industry describes four general categories: action, role playing, strategy, and simulations. However, many games often have elements of each.

Action Games

Popular *entertainment* action games are often based on a story line where the player must pay close attention and use quick reflexes if they are to be successful in achieving the goals of the game. Often action games are called "first-person shooter" games, because the goal of the game is to kill or destroy as many virtual enemies or threats as possible. The view is from the first person's weapon and players use a gaming controller to move through the game environment, point at, and then shoot the enemies as they appear on the screen.

Researchers cite benefits of playing action games that include enhanced vision and speed of cognitive processing. However, playing a lot of action games might also have some negative effects. For example, because there is so much action, visual attention could be reduced or distracted, which might impact a student's ability to follow information that doesn't move as quickly, like paying attention to the teacher in class (Bavelier, et al., 2011).

Action games allow players to play in multiplayer environments and must use communication and collaboration skills to team up to play against other teams using a variety of weaponry. Players must work on collaboration strategies to make decisions and critically think about how they will beat their opponents. To help students transfer those skills into productive collaboration skills, it is vital to help them make connections to see how they might use them within a more constructive way. Although this type of action game might help students learn communication and collaborative skills, some have more educational applications than others.

For example, online math action games have players complete math problems in a specific amount of time. When successful, students are often given some kind of reward and often a more difficult next level to achieve. Math Interactives provides a variety of interactive math games for middle and high school students, including Statistics and Probability such as Central Tendency and Distribution. A quick Google search will yield many other online games. However, it is important to have an instructional strategy because some are better used for skill practice, rather than critical thinking or problem solving.

Role-Playing Games (RPG)

Entertainment role-playing games (RPGs) have moved from non-electronic *Dungeons and Dragons* games, to complex massively multiplayer online role-playing games (MMORPG). In RPGs, the story is really the foundation and players take on a role or actor within the story. Commercial RPGs are generally similar to action games in that warfare, conflict, and competition are elements. However, emphasis is placed on collaboration and cooperation as players often have to work together to achieve the games goals.

Commercial RPGs, such as *World of Warcraft* (Blizzard Entertainment, Inc., 2013), have been integrated into classrooms with some success for gains in academic objectives. Young and colleagues (2012) described how MMPORGs were used for language learning, stating: "Language allows players to negotiate meaning for action within the game context, and the power of video games for language learning is attributed to this grounded use of language in context" (p. 75).

Darfur Is Dying (MTVU, 2009) teaches students about the conflict in Darfur region of the Sudan by playing the role of a Darfurian who must keep his or her refugee camp functioning by foraging for water and escape being captured by the rebels. *Peacemaker* (Impact Games, 2012) teaches students about the Israeli-Palestinian conflict and has players choose to play either the

Israeli prime minister or the Palestinian president in trying to solve this age-old conflict.

Classcraft (Classcraft Studios Inc., 2014) is an online RPG designed after *World of Warcraft* but is designed to help teachers with their classroom management by improving students' engagement, performance, and leadership and collaboration skills. Students role play three different characters (i.e., Healer, Mage, or Warrior) and gain or lose points based on their actual classroom behavior and achievements. Teachers can sign up their class for free, but there are also upgrades for a paid subscription.

Strategy Games

Traditional strategy games, such as chess, are the foundation for today's video strategy type games. Like chess, players in these digital games use strategy or tactics to out-maneuver their opponents in single player, multiplayer, or massively multiplayer online versions. Players move their avatars, armies, troops, and equipment from a map or world view, which provides a more strategic perspective.

There are two types of strategy games, turn-based, where players take turns or real-time continuous play. Although some strategy games focus strictly on tactics where the player acts as a tactician to best use their combat troops in a specific battle, others include action elements as well. For example, *America's Army* (Department of Defense, 2015) requires a lot of tactical and strategic decisions moving troops around; it also includes a great deal of multiplayer first-person shooter style action.

Simulation Games

SimCity (Electronic Arts, 2014), which was first developed in the mid-1980s, provides a virtual environments where players build simulated cities and communities and has been integrated into science, technology, engineering, and math by classroom teachers. Today students can engage with others within the multiplayer global market. Other simulation games provide opportunities for players to engage with peers in a virtual environment where they create an avatar and navigate through a virtual world.

Second Life (Linden Research, 2015) allows nonprofit organizations, medical training, and educational institutions to create a virtual venue for meetings, courses, and training. Many schools have created *Second Life* virtual campuses where students meet, create, and interact. Simulations of this nature can provide opportunities for students to practice observational skills and decision making. Although simulations can be helpful, especially in critical learning environments, such as a surgeon in a medical trauma unit, they can also be used to help students learn to make appropriate academic and life decisions.

GAMIFICATION

Gamification is a term used for adding gaming elements to instruction, which can stimulate student engagement and learning when done properly. Tu, Sujo-Montes, and Yen (2015) provided a model for gamifying existing curriculum that includes goal setting, where players set goals for the game; player engagement, where players get a sense of their game personality (i.e., what motivates them, intrinsic or extrinsic); progressive design, where players get a sense of progress, through the cycle of motivation, action, and feedback; and environment building, where players work collaboratively in teams or communities.

The classic Decisions-Decisions: Environment by Tom Snyder Productions (Scholastic, 2015) combines simulation, scenario, and role playing. Students work in teams and play the role of mayor of a small town with an environmental problem. In the scenario, the town's water was being polluted, and the town's biggest employer is being accused. Acting as the mayor, students have to come to a consensus to identify and prioritize three goals: support the town's environment, support the town's economy, or get re-elected as mayor. This often required a rigorous discussion between teammates as to *why* they wanted to choose their priorities.

One might consider the Decisions-Decisions series as an example of the gamification of curriculum. First students set their goals for the game by setting their priorities. Although there wasn't an explicit player engagement element within this game design, students had to discuss the reasons for *why* they set the priorities as they did, thus identifying their gaming personality. There was also progressive design by providing an engagement loop of motivation, action, and feedback. Environment building was also an element as students worked collaboratively, having to negotiate their individual ideas about how best to decide each decision with their teammates.

Adding gamification elements of goal setting, player engagement, progressive design, and environment building to existing curriculum is also an option. Think about gamifying a unit by adding these elements: students set their curricular goals, students get a sense of what motivates them (i.e., intrinsic or extrinsic), students can gain a sense of their progress, and students build an environment and gain a sense of community by working together.

GAMIFYING RESOURCES

- The Gamification Guide for Teachers. http://elearningindustry.com/the-gamification-guide-for-teachers
- Gamifying My Classroom. http://gamifyingmyclass.com
- Get Your Game On: How to Build Curriculum Units Using the Video Game Model. http://www.edutopia.org/blog/gamification-game-based-learning-unit-andrew-miller
- Gamification at the Curriculum Level. http://www.trainingindustry.com/blog/blog-entries/gamification-at-the-curriculum-level.aspx
- Gamification: Games and Curriculum. TEQ: It's All About Learning http://www.teq.com/blog/2015/06/gamification-games-curriculum-part-5-6/#.VbFfpflD5ko

SCENARIO: LEARNING WITH GAMES—WHAT'S THE REAL STORY

Jorge is an eighth-grade social studies teacher at a fairly progressive school that has many technology resources. He had been thinking about integrating a computer simulation game since reading an article on using *Civilization V* (Take-Two Interactive Software, 2010) to teach history (Blades, 2013). He found it interesting that having his students use the game might provide a good foundation for discussions on the accuracy of historical accounts, and how the law of accelerating returns describes how major historical events build on previous events, thus shortening the time between events, and decided to try integrating it into his curriculum.

Before beginning, however, he thought it best to discuss his idea with his principal and his fellow teachers. They gave him some good advice, suggesting that he do some research to find out what experiences others might have had. In doing so, he discovered that there were a couple of cautions in using *Civilization V*.

The game provided history events as embedded within context, but not necessarily historically linear because there are historical elements that may not be accurate, out of place, and or changed based on strategic decisions that students might make. Also, strategic games are not for everyone and some of his students might not engage to the level that he expected. The ESRB rating is for Everyone 10+ but does list "Drug References, Mild Language, Suggestive Themes and Violence," and *Civilization V* is a fairly complex and detailed game.

He decided to move forward because he believed that he understood the limitations of the game, but most importantly, believed that his students were at the appropriate grade level and ability. He designed a unit to use the off-the-shelf strategy game *Civilization V* in a way that supported his students engaging in the Inquiry Arc outlined in Dimension 3 within the C3 Framework (National Council for the Social Studies [NCSS], 2013). As they would go through the game, they would make strategic decisions based on what the students believed would be best for the citizens and culture at the time, but expecting that they would be basing those decisions from their twenty-first-century perspective.

He also had them research actual historical events that could then be compared and contrasted with their strategic decisions and consequences. By having his students do research on actual historical events, play *Civilization V* where they make strategic decisions that could well vary from the actual historical events, and then compare and contrast these two, Jorge believed that their discussions would help students learn about historical civilizations by examining elements of civilizations that made them great, and how history might have changed given different strategic decisions.

Through their engagement Jorge believed his students would be meeting the Inquiry Arc outlined in Dimension 2: Perspectives and Causation and Argumentation within the C3 Framework. Specifically, he wanted his students to be able to:

- D2.His.4.6-8. Analyze multiple factors that influenced the perspectives of people during different historical eras
- D2.His.5.6-8. Explain how and why perspectives of people have changed over time
- D2.His.14.6-8. Explain multiple causes and effects of events and developments in the past
- D2.His.15.6-8. Evaluate the relative influence of various causes of events and developments in the past

Although Jorge believed that his students were ready to engage in this unit, he was a bit concerned because this was the first time he'd integrated a video game into his classroom. To begin, he selected one target civilization from historically based civilizations that he'd planned to cover that term. He also decided to provide a great deal of structure because he believed the structure to help ensure that students would be supported in being successful. His structure included organizing his students into teams, which he decided might help alleviate the caution that strategy games are not necessarily for all students.

Jorge grouped his students in teams of three and assigned roles for the tasks of leader, historian/scribe, and tactician according to how he best felt each student would be successful. He then met with all students assigned to each role to outline their tasks and suggested that if they needed some additional help or suggestions that they should feel free to ask him but also talk with their like-role classmates.

During play, each role took responsibility for specific tasks. The leader was responsible for decisions based on the advice received from the other two team members. The historian/scribe was responsible for gathering facts and taking notes, in particular, of how the game deviated from history. The tactician was responsible for providing tactical advice to the leader based on historical events or strategies based on predicted advantageous outcomes, such as relative location of resources, allies, or foes.

Each team took turns on the game computer while the other teams used other computers and text resources to gather additional information about the civilization and historical events. Once the game was completed, each team created and presented a final multimedia (PowerPoint) report that outlined the game play in terms of alignment (or misalignment) to history, achievements their civilization gained or lost, and an examination and assessment of crucial decisions. Each team member was responsible for his or her own section of the report.

Jorge decided to assess his student on this unit in a couple of ways. As a formative assessment he would observe how each student and team engaged in the unit (both game play and class discussions) and write down anecdotal notes on his observations. Although he decided not to grade them on their engagement, he believed that he could use it for his own understandings of how well integrating the game into his curriculum went.

He decided that he would use the final report as part of the summative assessment. Each team would receive team points for the final report so he created a rubric for various levels of achievement that included rows for multimedia presentation; creativity; historical accuracy in terms of events and details of civilization achievements; and grammar and spelling. In addition, each student would receive points for their individual section so he created a rubric for various levels of achievement that included rows for completeness of their section, participation, and grammar and spelling.

The final report could assess the group's findings and the individual group member's participation. However, Jorge also wanted to be able to assess each individual student's achievement of the specific C3 Framework Dimension 2: Perspectives and Causation and Argumentation outcomes. Therefore, each student was required to write a reflection paper in which they answered the following:

- What were the factors that influenced the perspectives of people during this historical era? (D2.His.4.6-8)
- How and why do their perspectives differ from yours of today? (D2.His.5.6-8)

- Identify an historical event, describe what caused it and the effects it had on the civilization. (D2.His.14.6-8)
- Describe what influence the causes of that event had on the development of that civilization. (D2.His.15.6-8)

SUMMARY

The purpose of this chapter is to provide an overview or foundation of research, the types of video games, and the issues or concerns when games are integrated into the classroom. It's important to remember that research on video game play for learning suggests that it is a complex topic. Although some suggest that video games can become an addiction or playing violent video games can enhance violent behavior, there are others who suggest that video game play in the classroom motivates student engagement and provides opportunities for technology enhanced learning.

In addition, gamification and the elements that help educators gamify curriculum is also discussed. The scenario provided an example of how a commercial off-the-shelf game could be integrated into social studies curriculum to help students achieve national standards. It is important to remember, however, that within this scenario, the teacher took a great deal of time investigating and preparing before designing his unit to make sure it was a solid instructional method. Given the research and public opinion of many video games, this could be especially important when integrating games into the curriculum.

Although the chapter provides ways to integrate gaming into the classroom, as with all instructional strategies that integrate digital tools, it's important to have a foundation that supports students learning. In other words, integrating digital games might well be cool or fun, but the main purpose is to help students learn.

REFERENCES

Anderson, C. A., Shibuya, A., Ihori, N., Swing, E. L., Bushman, B. J., Sakamoto, A., Rothstein, H. R., and Saleem, M. (2010). Violent video game effects on aggression, empathy, and prosocial behavior in eastern and western countries: A meta-analytic review. *Psychological bulletin*, *136*(2), 151.

Bavelier, D., Green, S., Han, D., Renshaw, P., Merzenich, M., and Gentile, D. (2011). Brains on video games. *Nature Reviews Neuroscience, 12*(12), 763–768.

Bethesda Softworks LLC. (2015). *Skyrim*. Retrieved from http://www.elderscrolls.com/skyrim/

Blades, R. (2013). Gaming and history: *Civilization V* and the law of accelerating returns. Humanities, arts, science, technology alliance and collaboratory. Retrieved from http://www.hastac.org/blogs/rblades/2013/01/06/gaming-and-history-civilization-v-and-law-accelerating-returns.

Blizzard Entertainment, Inc. (2013). Beginner's Guide, Game Guide, *World of Warcraft*. Retrieved from http://us.battle.net/wow/en/game/guide/

Classcraft Studios Inc. (2014). Make learning an adventure. Retrieved from http://www.classcraft.com.

Dai, D. Y., and Wind, A. P. (2011). Computer games and opportunity to learn: Implications from low socioeconomic backgrounds. In S. Tobias and J. D. Fletcher (eds.), *Computer games and instruction* (pp. 477–500). Charlotte, NC: Information Age Publishing.

Department of Defense. (2015). *America's army*. Retrieved from http://www.americasarmy.com/.

Electronic Arts Inc. (2014). *SimCity*. Retrieved from http://www.simcity.com.

Grüsser, S. M., Thalemann, R., and Griffiths, M. D. (2006). Excessive computer game playing: Evidence for addiction and aggression? *CyberPsychology & Behavior, 10* (2), 290–292.

Houghton Mifflin Harcourt. (2015). *Oregon Trail*. Retrieved from http://www.hmhco.com/at-home/featured-shops/the-learning-company/oregon-trail.

Impact Games. (2012). PeaceMaker: Play the news, solve the puzzle. Retrieved from http://www.impactgames.com/peacemaker.php.

Kirschner, P.A., Sweller, J., and Clark, R. E. (2006). Why minimal guidance during instruction does not work: An analysis of the failure of constructivist, discovery, problem-based, experiential, and inquiry-based teaching. *Educational Psychologist. 41*, 75–76.

Klahr, D., and Nigam, M. (2004). The equivalence of learning paths in early science instruction. *Psychological Science, 15* (10), 661–667.

Linden Research Inc. (2015). *Second Life*. Retrieved from http://secondlife.com

Mayer, R. E. (2004). Should there be a three-strikes rule against pure discovery learning? The case for guided methods of instruction. *American Psychologist, 59*, 14–19.

MTVU. (2013). *Darfur Is Dying*: Play mtvU's Darfur refugee game for change. Retrieved from http://www.darfurisdying.com/aboutgame.html.

National Council for the Social Studies (NCSS). (2013). The College, Career, and Civic Life (C3) Framework for Social Studies State Standards: Guidance for Enhancing Rigor of K–12 Civics, Economics, Geography and History. Silver Spring, MD: Author.

Resnick, M. (2004). Edutainment? No thanks. I prefer playful learning. *Associazione Civita Report on Edutainment, 14*.

Scholastic. (2015). *Decisions-decisions: Environment by Tom Snyder Productions*. Retrieved from http://teacher.scholastic.com/products/tomsnyder.htm.

Schwartz, K. (2014). Bypassing the textbook: Video games transform social studies curriculum. Retrieved from http://ww2.kqed.org/mindshift/2014/01/16/forget-the-textbook-video-games-as-social-studies-content/.

Take-Two Interactive Software. (2010). *Civilization V*. Retrieved from http://www.civilization5.com/.

Tu, C. H., Sujo-Montes, L. E., and Yen, C. J. (2015). Gamification for learning. In R. Papa (ed.), *Media Rich Instruction: Connecting curriculum to all learners* (pp. 203–217). New York: Springer International Publishing.

Van Eck, R. (2009). A guide to integrating COTS games into your classroom. *Handbook of research on effective electronic gaming in education, 1*.

Young, M. F., Slota, S. T., Cutter, A. B., Jalette, G., Mullin, G., Lai, B., Simeoni, Z., Tran, M., Yukhymenko, M. (2012). Our princess is in another castle: A review of trends in serious gaming for education. *Review of Educational Research, 82* (1), 61–89.

Yousafzai, S., Hussain, Z., and Griffiths, M. (2013). Social responsibility in online videogaming: What should the videogame industry do? *Addiction Research & Theory*, 1–5.

Index

academic standards, 27–32; Common Core English Language Arts Standards (CCELA), 30, 51, 72, 75, 77, 80; Common Core issues, 31; Common Core Mathematics Standards, 30–31, 79; National Curriculum Standards for Social Studies (NCSS), 29, 51, 53, 85–86, 108, 121–122; National Educational Technology Standards (NETS), 32; Next Generation Science Standards (NGSS), 29, 34. *See also* assessment
American Federation of Teachers (AFT), 30
appropriate use policy, 56
assessment: assessment of group work, 35–36, 36; formative assessment, 33–34, 38, 63, 73, 74, 123; individual content assessment rubric, 37; objectives, 28, 34, 62, 85, 115, 118; outcomes, 27, 28–29, 31, 34, 34–53, 35, 36, 38, 51, 80, 88, 99, 123; performance indicators, 28, 32, 33, 34, 36–38, 38, 72; summative assessment, 32, 34, 35, 36–38, 63, 74–75, 123; team checklist, 36, 38. *See also* academic standards
asynchronous, 68. *See also* synchronous
Audacity, 47, 52, 96. *See also* open-source software

Berne Convention treaty, 58

Blackboard, 69, 72. *See also* learning management systems
blogs, 38, 69, 97. *See also* digital tools; communication

Calibre, 98, 98–99, 100. *See also* open-source software
case-based learning, 19, 20, 103
Chromebook, 46
cognitive map, ix, 6, 73, 91, 92, 92–94, 93. *See also* semantic map
Collaboration, ix, 6, 7, 19, 21, 30, 61, 67–75, 86, 98, 109, 110, 112, 118, 119
cooperative learning, 21–22, 35
computer literacy, 7
computer-based instruction (CBI), 8
computer-based software, 46, 53
critical thinking, ix, 11, 24, 103–104, 111
cyberbullying, 55, 57, 61–62, 63, 64

DataStudio, 81
digital tools: audio creation and manipulation, 96; communication, ix, 7, 9, 12, 56, 56–57, 64, 67–69, 71–72, 72, 75; data collection and analysis, ix, 77–78, 81–82, 83–85, 89; exploration, 104, 105, 111; image creation and manipulation, 95; games for learning, 115–117; logical thinking, 103, 106, 111; planning, 10, 110; presentations, vii, 7, 32, 46, 47, 52, 55, 62–63, 74–75,

91, 94, 95, 97, 103, 106, 123; publishing, ix, 9, 11, 12, 64, 91–92, 94–95, 97, 99, 100, 105, 112; multimedia editing, 95; spreadsheet, 46, 47, 71, 73, 74, 80, 82, 83–84, 84, 85, 105; video creation and manipulation, 96; visualization, 6, 9, 91–92, 93–94; word processing, 11, 46, 47

digital citizenship,– 55–56, 60, 61, 62, 63–64, 68, 75; access, 50, 52, 53, 55–56, 56, 59–60, 61, 62, 63–64; commerce, 56, 57, 61, 64; communication, 56, 56–57, 64, 68; etiquette, 56, 61, 68; ethics, 58; fair use, 57, 58–59; health and wellness, 56, 57; law, 55, 56, 57, 58–59, 61, 64; plagiarism, 58, 63; rights and responsibilities, 55, 56, 58, 61, 64, 68

Dropbox, 83, 85, 112. *See also* file storage and management

e-book, 96–97, 98–100
Edmodo, 69. *See also* learning management systems
English language learners, 70, 93
email, 46, 47, 67, 68, 69, 82, 97, 112. *See also* digital tools; for communication
ePals, 61, 73, 82, 97
e-pub format, 97, 98
e-readers, 98

Facebook, 70, 97
file storage and management: good data-saving habits, 49–50; file naming and management, 48, 49–50, 83; local storage, 48; network or cloud storage, 49

game-based learning, 116–117; action games, 117–118; first-person shooter games, 117, 119; gamification, 120–121; massively multiplayer online role-playing games (MMORPG), 117, 118, 119; role-playing games (RPGs), 118–119; simulation games, 9, 117, 119, 121; strategy games, 119, 122
general public licensed, 57, 59. *See also* open-source software

Geometer's Sketchpad, 6, 105
Gimp, 47, 52, 95. *See also* digital tools; image creation and manipulation
global digital citizenship. *See* digital citizenship
global education, 60
Glogster, 71
Google Apps : Classroom, 72; Docs, 46, 47, 49, 71, 72, 75, 82, 98; Drive, 83, 85; Forms, 73, 74, 80, 82, 83; Hangouts, 67; Search, 51, 118; Sites, 69, 72, 73, 98, 112; Slides, 62
graphic organizer. *See* cognitive map

iBook Author, 96, 99–100. *See also* digital tools; publishing
iMovie, 96. *See also* digital tools; publishing
individual accountability, 22, 35–36, 64–112
inquiry-based learning, 19–20, 103
Inspiration, ix, 7, 92–94, 93. *See also* digital tools; planning
InspireData, 85. *See also* digital tools; data collection and analysis
Instagram, 68, 70
instructional decisions, 3, 12, 15, 20, 24
instructional strategies, ix, 10, 15, 19, 20, 24, 25, 89, 103–104, 112
International Reading Association (IRA), 29
International Society for Technology in Education (ISTE), 28, 32, 62

Kidspiration, 92. *See also* digital tools; planning
KWL chart, 91–92, 92

learning management systems (LMS), 69
LibreOffice, 47, 52, 85. *See also* open-source software
Linux, 44, 47, 50. *See also* open-source software
LOGO, 12, 106

Microsoft Office, 46, 47
Microsoft OneDrive, 47, 71, 83
Mindtools, 11–12

Moodle, 69. *See also* learning management systems

National Council of Teachers of English (NCTE), 29, 30
National Council of Teachers of Mathematics (NCTM), 29, 30
National Education Association (NEA), 30
No Child Left Behind (NCLB), 27

open-source software, 46, 47–48, 51, 52, 57, 59, 69, 94, 95, 98, 99

Partnership for Assessment of Readiness for College and Careers (PARCC), 31
personally meaningful products/artifacts, 6
perspective of learning, 3–4, 4, 7; constructionism, 5–6; constructivism, 3–5, 12; constructivist perspective, 5, 9, 10; distributed constructionism, 6; objectivism, 3–5, 12; objectivist perspective, 5, 9; objectivist–constructivist continuum, 4, 4–5, 5, 12–13; student-centered, vii, ix, x, 5, 12, 15, 18–19, 20, 21, 24, 38, 91, 111, 116, 117; teacher-centered C01bf2
place value, 31
podcast, 97
point of tension, 15, 17–19, 21, 24–25
positive group interdependence, 22, 64, 112
problem-based learning (PBL), 20–21, 103, 104, 107, 111; characteristics of, 20; ill-structured problem, 20, 104
problem solving, ix, 7, 20, 82, 103–104, 111, 115, 118
project-based learning, 19, 104
Purdue's Online Writing Lab (OWL), 58

qualitative data, 80–81, 82, 89
quantitative data, 79–80, 81, 85, 86–87, 89

scaffolds, 5, 18, 19, 20–21, 23, 24, 25, 79, 107, 111; hard scaffolds, 23; soft scaffolds, 23, 24
scenario-based learning, 105, 108

scenarios, 8, 12, 62, 63, 103, 104–105, 111
scientific data collection devices, 81. *See also* digital tools; data collection and analysis
semantic map, 92. *See also* cognitive map
server-based software, 46, 47, 48
simulations, 9, 18, 103, 104, 105–106, 106, 111, 117, 119
Skype, 61, 67, 71
SMART Board, vii, 73
smartphone, vii, 7, 55, 81, 82, 87, 97
social media, 7, 57, 61, 62, 63, 68, 70, 75, 97
special needs learners, 50, 53, 60
StarLOGO, 106
student response systems (SRS), 68
synchronous, 68, 71, 75. *See also* asynchronous

tablets, vii, 71, 82, 97, 98, 99; Android, 82, 97, 99; iPad, vii, 50, 81, 82, 96–97, 98, 99
technology operations: basic input/output system (BIOS), 44; operating system (OS), 7, 43, 44, 47, 50, 59, 60, 95–96; central processing unit (CPU), 45; local area network (LAN), 49; multistore memory model, 43, 44; random access memory (RAM), 45; removable storage, 48–49; wide area network (WAN), 49
Twitter, 61, 68, 70, 97
type I applications, 10–11
type II applications, 10, 11

Ubuntu, 47, 50. *See also* open-source software
US Copyright Office, 58

Vodcast, 97
voiceover screen reader, 50

Web 2.0, 70–71
wikis, 69. *See also* digital tools; communication

About the Author

As an educator for more than thirty-five years, J. Michael Blocher, PhD has taught in a variety of classrooms. His teaching experiences span from third-grade elementary classroom teacher to doctoral dissertation chair. His research interests include learner engagement in online learning environments, technology integration into the curriculum, technology-based instructional media, and gaming for learning. He has published articles and book chapters and presented numerous papers on topics within the field of Educational Technology nationally and internationally.

Blocher currently serves as professor of educational technology in Northern Arizona University's College of Education where he teaches face-to-face and online undergraduate, masters, and doctoral level courses. He especially enjoys teaching the *computers in the classroom* course for undergraduate students in Northern Arizona University's teacher preparation program. Over the years, he has noticed that his students have changed and now come into his class with considerable technology skills. However, they often struggle with planning lessons where technology is used by the students in ways that support their achievement of academic standards. This text was written in response to his desire to provide foundational information and examples of how teachers can design lessons and units where their students use today's digital tools to help them construct knowledge.

www.ingramcontent.com/pod-product-compliance
Lightning Source LLC
Chambersburg PA
CBHW030143240426
43672CB00005B/243